KB054830

남북한 유엔 가입

총회결안 추진 및 기본입장 각서

남북한 유엔 가입

총회결안 추진 및 기본입장 각서

한국학술정보

| 머리말

유엔 가입은 대한민국 정부 수립 이후 중요한 숙제 중 하나였다. 한국은 1949년을 시작으로 여러 차례 유엔 가입을 시도했으나, 상임이사국인 소련의 거부권 행사에 번번이 부결되고 말았다. 북한도 마찬가지로, 1949년부터 유엔 가입을 시도했으나 상임이사국들의 반대에 매번 가로막혔다. 서로가 한반도의 유일한 합법 정부라 주장하는 당시 남북한은 어디까지나 상대측을 배제하고 단독으로 유엔에 가입하려 했으며, 이는 국제적인 냉전 체제와 맞물려 어느 쪽도 원하는 바를 성취하지 못하게 만들었다. 하지만 1980년대를 지나며 냉전 체제가 이완되면서 변화가 생긴다. 한국은 북방 정책을 통해 국제적 여건을 조성하고, 남북한 고위급 회담 등에서 남북한 유엔 동시 가입 등을 강력히 설득한다. 이런 외교적 노력이 1991년 열매를 맺어, 제46차 유엔총회를 통해 한국과 북한은 유엔 회원국이 될 수 있었다.

본 총서는 외교부에서 작성하여 30여 년간 유지한 남북한 유엔 가입 관련 자료를 담고 있다. 한국의 유엔 가입 촉구를 위한 총회결의한 추진 검토, 세계 각국을 대상으로 한 지지 교섭 과정, 국내외 실무 절차 진행, 채택 과정 및 향후 대응, 관련 홍보 및 언론 보도까지 총 16권으로 구성되었다. 전체 분량은 약 8천 쪽에 이른다.

2024년 3월
한국학술정보(주)

| 일러두기

· 본 총서에 실린 자료는 2022년 4월과 2023년 4월에 각각 공개한 외교문서 4,827권, 76만 여 쪽 가운데 일부를 발췌한 것이다.

· 각 권의 제목과 순서는 공개된 원본을 최대한 반영하였으나, 주제에 따라 일부는 적절히 변경하였다.

· 원본 자료는 A4 판형에 맞게 축소하거나 원본 비율을 유지한 채 A4 페이지 안에 삽입 하였다. 또한 현재 시점에선 공개되지 않아 '공란'이란 표기만 있는 페이지 역시 그대로 실었다.

· 외교부가 공개한 문서 각 권의 첫 페이지에는 '정리 보존 문서 목록'이란 이름으로 기록물 종류, 일자, 명칭, 간단한 내용 등의 정보가 수록되어 있으며, 이를 기준으로 0001번부터 번호가 매겨져 있다. 이는 삭제하지 않고 총서에 그대로 수록하였다.

· 보고서 내용에 관한 더 자세한 정보가 필요하다면, 외교부가 온라인상에 제공하는 『대한 민국 외교사료요약집』1991년과 1992년 자료를 참조할 수 있다.

| 차례

정 리 보 존 문 서 목 록

기록물종류	일반공문서철	등록번호	2020070024	등록일자	2020-07-13
분류번호	731.12	국가코드		보존기간	영구
명 칭	남북한 유엔가입, 1991.9.17. 전41권				
생 산 과	국제연합1과	생산년도	1990~1991	담당그룹	
권 차 명	V.4 한국의 유엔가입 촉구 총회결의안 추진 검토, 1990				
내용목차	* 거부권이 예상되는 안전보장이사회 보다 다수결의 원칙이 적용되는 유엔총회에서 한국의 유엔가입 문제 토론 및 결의안 제출 방안 검토				

0001

아국의 유엔가입 촉구 총회결의안 추진 문제

1990. 4.

0002

목   차

Ⅰ. 문제의 제기

Ⅱ. 총회결의안 추진문제 검토

Ⅲ. 북한측의 예상반응

첨 부 : 1. 관련 검토사항

2. 88년 아국대표 총회연설 추진시 표세 최종분석

3. 과거 아국가입 촉구 총회결의 사본 (4건)

0003

Ⅰ. 문제의 제기

o 아국 외교정책의 숙원과제인 유엔가입은 유엔 안전보장이사회
  에서 거부권을 가지고 있는 상임이사국중 소련과 중국의 부정
  적인 태도로 실현되지 못하고 있음.

o 최근 국제사회의 전반적인 평화, 협력분위기와 아국의 국제적
  위상 부각 및 북방정책을 통한 동구권과의 관계개선으로 유엔
  가입 실현을 위한 분위기는 과거 어느때보다 개선되었으나,
  소.중, 특히 중국의 거부권 행사 가능성은 상존하며, 이들
  국가의 긍정적 태도 변화가 확인되지 않은 상황에서 아국의
  유엔가입 실현은 사실상 어려운 상대임.

o 따라서, 소.중에 대하여 아국가입문제에 거부권을 행사하지
  않도록 설득하는 것이 현시점에서 아국유엔가입 실현의 관건
  이라고 할 수 있음.

o 이같은 상황에서, 특정국가의 거부권이 없어 다수결의 원칙이
  적용되는 유엔총회에 아국의 유엔가입을 촉구하는 견의안을
  제출하는 문제에 관하여 그 장단점 및 관련사항을 검토코자 함.

0004

Ⅱ. 총회 결의안 추진문제 검토

1. ~~장~~ 점승정정인촉비는

   ○ 아국 유엔가입 지지 기반 확인

   - 다수 유엔회원국의 찬성으로 결의를 채택시켜 국제
     사회에서의 아국 유엔가입에 대한 지지기반을 확인하고,
     지지규모의 세과시가 가능함.

   북한등 투표되도 변화기대

   ○ 소.중의 거부권 부재 및 ~~거권~~ 가능 *변화를 할수있지 비료?*
   - 안보리와 달리 소.중이 거부권을 행사할 수 없음 *반대하더라도 결의안은 포기토록 시켜두었음*
   - 동 총회결의안 채택이 아국 유엔가입을 실현시키는
     으로   의   을 데
     것이 아니므로 ~~소.중으로서도 거권이 가능함.~~

   → 소.중, 특히 소련을 기권, 투표불참 등
   (반대로 통과하지 않을 가능성이 있었음)

   ○ 아국 유엔가입 실현 분위기 고조

   - 압도적 다수로 채택될시 아국 유엔가입의 당위성이
     국제사회에서 뚜렷이 부각됨으로써 아국가입 촉구
     여론을 환기시킬 수 있음.

   - 소.중에 대하여 추후 거부권 행사를 자제하도록하~~노~~ *근제 정인*
     압력으로 작용할 수 있음.

   부정적측면?
2. ~~단점~~

   ○ 유엔에서의 남북한 대결 재연

   - 북한의 강력한 반대 책동이 예상되며, 이로 인하여
     남북한간의 위대결이
     유엔~~에서~~ ~~대결~~ 상대자 불가피함. (표결 북한 예상 반응 참고)
   - 이는 7.7선언이후 아국의 화해지향 정책과 배치되는 *문순함*
     인상을 줄 수 있음.

   *유엔에서 남북한의 동시 지향을 밝혀 온 우리의
   입장과 모순됨*

0005

(상단 손글씨)
아울러 유엔 가입문제는 군사적 발전의 위협을 가족안[...]
[...]에게 있음[...] [...]축들이 太泰한 자세 [...]
[...]계 경대국 들의 태도를 의식하여 특별한 태도에 아양[...]
성향이 많음.

o **대다수 찬성표 확보를 위한 외교적 부담**

- 단순한 결의의 채택만으로는 아국유연가입 지지 기반
  확인의 의미가 적으므로, 다수국가의 찬성확보를 위한
  외교적 부담이 높음. *전에*

  (결의안 체택시에도 다수가 기권하고 단순히 찬성이
  반대보다 많은 경우 의미 별무)

- 만일, 결의안채택이 실패하는 경우 외교적 손상이 큼.

o **총회결의와 ~~아국~~ 유엔가입 실현과의 직접적 연계성 부재**

- 아국의 유엔가입문제를 안보리에서 재심하여 줄것을
  촉구하는 내용의 유엔총회결의는 이미 과거 4차례
  채택된 바 있으나, 실질적 효과는 의문시됨
  (손글씨) 안보리의 재심, 지속적 [...]으로

o ~~북방외교에 대한 부정적 영향 가능~~ *(손글씨) 가입실현과 진실 연계 되지 않음*
  ~~총~~결의안 채택시에도 소 중에 대한 이같은 공개적 압력이
  바람직한가에 대한 비판이 가능함. ~~(관계개선에 부정적 영향 가능)~~
  (우측 손글씨) 는 소,중의 가입이 의미로서 로 [...]순적 스러도 [...]로기 [...]방함

o **절차적 문제**
  (손글씨) 서 우리 대국여망 [...]임으로

- 아국가입문제가 1949년 이래 안보리에 계류된 상태이므로
  동 총회결의안 추진에 절차적 하자는 없겠으나, 우방국
  들은 아국에게 안보리가 마지막으로 아국가입 문제를
  다룬 1975년 이후 국제정세가 크게 달라졌으므로 총회
  결의안 추진에 앞서 우선 가입문제에 1차적 책임을 갖고
  있는 안보리에 재신청을 먼저 추진해 볼 것을 제기할
  가능성이 있음.

0006

3. 결 론

   o 상기와 같은 장단점을 고려할때, 아국 유엔가입 촉구
     총회 결의안 추진은 현시점에서 득보다는 실이 많은
     것으로 판단됨.

   o 동 추진문제는 유엔 핵심우방국 협의회 제 2차회의
     (5월초 개최 예정)시에도 토의 예정이므로, 동 회의
     결과와 추후 관련 국제상황의 진전을 계속 검토하여 추후
     90.6.경 최종 결론을 내리는 것이 좋을 것으로 사료됨.

Ⅲ. 북한측의 예상 반응

1. 대응 결의안 제출

o 신규회원국 가입 의제하에서 남북한의 통일후 가입 또는
  단일 국호하의 가입을 촉구하는 결의안 제출 가능

o 한반도 문제를 부활시키는 새로운 의제(예 : 1975년
  한국문제 관련 결의의 이행)를 상정, 대응 결의안 제출
  가능

o 아측 결의안 내용을 희석시켜, 효과면에서 무의미하게
  만드는 수정안 추진 가능

o 남북한 결의안을 모두 철회토록 유도 노력 가능

2. 아측 결의안 부결 책동

o 아측결의안을 부결시키기 위하여 유엔 회원국들의 반대
  또는 기권 유도 노력

o 비동맹 과격세력등 북한 동조국가 총동원 예상

0008

(첨 부)

I. 관련 검토사항

1. 과거 사례

49.4.8.   안보리, 아국가입 권고결의안 부결(소련 거부권행사)

49.11.22.   총회, 한국가입신청 재심의를 안보리에 요청하는
           결의 채택 〈결의 296 G(IV)〉

50.12.4.   총회, 한국포함 9개국 가입신청의 계속 검토를
           안보리에 요청하는 결의 채택 〈결의 495 (V)〉

55.12.8.   총회, 18개국 가입권고 공동결의안 채택

           〈결의 918(X)〉
           * 쿠바는 한국, 베트남을 포함한 수정결의안을
             제출했다가 철회

57.2.28.   총회, 한국가입신청 재심의를 안보리에 요청하는
           결의 채택 〈결의 1017 A(XII)〉

57.9.9.   안보리, 한국가입에 관한 8개국 공동결의안 부결
           (소련 거부권행사)

57.10.25. 총회, 한국의 유엔가입 타당성 재확인 결의 채택
           〈결의 1144 A(XII)〉

0003

아국대표 총회 연설 지지국 현황 분석

(최 종)

* 지지확실 81. 지지가능 10 (계 91)

반대 36. 불확실 22. 기권 10

(*는 운영위원국)

88. 9. 22. 국제연합과

구 분	지 지 확 실	지 지 가 능	불 확 실	반 대	기 권
보충의제 공동제안국 (10)	일본, 미국*, 카나다*, 코스타리카, 콜롬비아, 영국*, 라이베리아, 시에라레온, 오만, 파라과이 (10)				
핵심우방국 (6)	방글라데시,싱가폴, 덴마크*, 케냐*, 코트디브와트*(5)	에쿠아돌*, (1)			
아 주 (23)	태국*, 파키스탄, 필리핀,PNG, 휘지, 솔로몬아일랜드, 스리랑카, 말레이지아, 서사모아,부탄(10)	브루나이, 몰디브, 네팔* (3)	버마, 바누아투*, (2)	라오스, 몽고, 베트남, 중국*, 캄푸챠 (5)	인도, 인니, 사이 프러스* (3)
서구 및 기타 (19)	터키, 서독, 벨기에, 뉴질랜드, 호주, 희랍, 화란, 아일랜드, 몰타*, 놀웨이, 오지리, 룩셈부르크, 아이슬랜드, 불란서* (14)	폴투갈, 스페인, 이태리 (3)	스웨덴 (1)		핀랜드 (1)
중남미 (29)	알젠틴*, 도미니카 (공), 볼리비아*, 우루과이, 바하마, 트리니다드토바고, 칠레, 과테말라, 그레나다, 수리남, 세인트빈센트*, 도미니카(연), 엘살바돌*,아이티, 안티구아바부다, 세인트키츠네비스 멕시코, 파나마, 온두라스 (19)	바베이도스 (1)	페루,브라질, 자마이카, 베네수엘라, 벨리즈, 세인트루시아, (6)	니카라과, 쿠바 (2)	가이 아나 (1)

0010

구 분	지지확실	지지가능	불확실	반 대	기 권
중 동 (21)	바레인*, 카탈, 튀니지, 요르단, 쿠웨이트*, 수단*, 사우디, 이라크, 모로코, UAE, 북예멘 (11)		모리타니아, 레바논, 이스라엘, 리비아 (4)	남예멘, 시리아, 알제리, 아프가니스탄, (4)	이란, 이집트 (2)
아프리카 (40)	자이르, 감비아, 나이제리아, 니제, 카메룬, 가봉, 소말리아, 적도기니, 모리셔스, 스와질랜드*, 중앙아, 상토메프린시페* (12)	지부티, 말라위 (2)	레소토, 루안다, 보츠와나, 코모로, 캅베르데, 남아공, 모잠비크, 챠드, 우간다 (9)	기네, 부르키나파소, 이디오피아, 세이쉘, 앙골라, 잠비아, 콩고, 짐바브웨, 토고, 부룬디, 탄자니아*, 말리, 베냉, 마다가스칼 (14)	기네비소*, 세네갈, 가나 (3)
동 구 (11)				알바니아, 불가리아, 체코, 동독, 폴란드*, 루마니아, 소련*, 유고*, 헝가리, 백러시아, 우크라이나 (11)	
계 (159)	81	10	22	36	10

0011

Charter for the maintenance of international peace and security as well as the duties assigned by the Charter or by the General Assembly or by any Security Council to other Councils or to any committee or commission. The Interim Committee shall not consider any matter of which the Security Council is seized and which the latter has not submitted to the General Assembly;

5. The rules of procedure governing the proceedings of the Interim Committee and such sub-committees and commissions as it may set up shall be those adopted by the Interim Committee on 9 January 1948[8] as amended by the Interim Committee on 31 March 1949,[9] with such changes and additions as the Interim Committee may deem necessary, provided that they are not inconsistent with any provisions of this resolution. The Interim Committee shall hold the first meeting of its annual session at the Headquarters of the United Nations within six weeks from the date of the conclusion or adjournment of any regular session of the General Assembly. The date of the first meeting of each session of the Interim Committee shall be determined by the Chairman elected during the previous session, or by the head of his delegation, in consultation with the Secretary-General, who shall notify the members of the Committee accordingly. At the opening meeting, the Chairman elected during the previous session of the Committee or the head of his delegation shall preside until the Interim Committee has elected a Chairman. The Interim Committee shall meet as and when it deems necessary for the conduct of its business. No new credentials shall be required for representatives who were duly accredited to the Interim Committee during its previous session;

6. The Secretary-General shall provide the necessary facilities and assign appropriate staff as required for the work of the Interim Committee, its sub-committees and commissions.

250th plenary meeting,
21 November 1949.

296 (IV). Admission of new Members

A

The General Assembly,

Noting from the special report[10] of the Security Council on the reconsideration of the application of Austria for membership in the United Nations that nine members of the Security Council, on 13 September 1949, supported a draft resolution recommending the admission to the United Nations of Austria, but that no recommendation was made to the General Assembly because of the opposition of one permanent member,

Deeming it important to the development of the United Nations that all applicant States which possess the qualifications for membership set forth in Article 4 of the Charter should be admitted,

Considering that the opposition to the application of Austria was based on grounds not included in Article 4 of the Charter,

Recalling the recommendation of the General Assembly in resolution 197 (III) A[11] of 8 December 1948 that each member of the Security Council and of the General Assembly, in exercising its vote on the admission of new Members, should act in accordance with the advisory opinion[12] of the International Court of Justice of 28 May 1948, which declared that a State was not juridically entitled to make its consent to the admission dependent on conditions not expressly provided by paragraph 1 of Article 4,

1. *Reaffirms* its determination that Austria is, in its judgment, a peace-loving State within the meaning of Article 4 of the Charter, is able and willing to carry out the obligations of the Charter, and should therefore be admitted to membership in the United Nations;

2. *Requests* the Security Council to reconsider the application of Austria, in the light of this determination of the General Assembly.

252nd plenary meeting,
22 November 1949.

B

The General Assembly,

Noting from the special report[13] of the Security Council on the reconsideration of the application of Ceylon for membership in the United Nations that nine members of the Security Council, on 13 September 1949, supported a draft resolution recommending the admission to the United Nations of Ceylon, but that no recommendation was made to the General Assembly because of the opposition of one permanent member,

Deeming it important to the development of the United Nations that all applicant States which possess the qualifications for membership set forth in Article 4 of the Charter should be admitted,

Considering that the opposition to the application of Ceylon was based on grounds not included in Article 4 of the Charter,

Recalling the recommendation of the General Assembly in resolution 197 (III) A of 8 December 1948 that each member of the Security Council and of the General Assembly, in exercising its vote on the admission of new Members, should act in accordance with the advisory opinion of the International Court of Justice of 28 May 1948, which declared that a State was not juridically entitled to make its consent to the admission dependent on conditions not expressly provided by paragraph 1 of Article 4,

1. *Determines* that Ceylon is, in its judgment, a peace-loving State within the meaning of Article 4 of the Charter, is able and willing to carry out the obligations of the Charter, and should therefore be admitted to membership in the United Nations;

---

[8] See document A/AC.18/8.
[9] See document A/AC.18/8/Rev.1.
[10] See *Official Records of the fourth session of the General Assembly, Annex to the Ad Hoc Political Committee,* document A/982.
[11] See *Official Records of the third session of the General Assembly, Part I, Resolutions,* page 30.

[12] See *Admission of a State to the United Nations (Charter, Article 4), Advisory Opinion: I.C.J. Reports 1948,* page 57.
[13] See *Official Records of the fourth session of the General Assembly, Annex to the Ad Hoc Political Committee,* document A/982.

18

0012

2. *Requests* the Security Council to reconsider the application of Ceylon, in the light of this determination of the General Assembly.

252nd plenary meeting,
22 November 1949.

C

The General Assembly,

Noting from the special report[14] of the Security Council on the reconsideration of the application of Finland for membership in the United Nations that nine members of the Security Council, on 13 September 1949, supported a draft resolution recommending the admission to the United Nations of Finland, but that no recommendation was made to the General Assembly because of the opposition of one permanent member,

Deeming it important to the development of the United Nations that all applicant States which possess the qualifications for membership set forth in Article 4 of the Charter should be admitted,

Considering that the opposition to the application of Finland was based on grounds not included in Article 4 of the Charter,

Recalling the recommendation of the General Assembly in resolution 197 (III) A of 8 December 1948 that each member of the Security Council and of the General Assembly, in exercising its vote on the admission of new Members, should act in accordance with the advisory opinion of the International Court of Justice of 28 May 1948, which declared that a State was not juridically entitled to make its consent to the admission dependent on conditions not expressly provided by paragraph 1 of Article 4,

1. *Reaffirms* its determination that Finland is, in its judgment, a peace-loving State within the meaning of Article 4 of the Charter, is able and willing to carry out the obligations of the Charter, and should therefore be admitted to membership in the United Nations;

2. *Requests* the Security Council to reconsider the application of Finland, in the light of this determination of the General Assembly.

252nd plenary meeting,
22 November 1949.

D

The General Assembly,

Noting from the special report[15] of the Security Council on the reconsideration of the application of Ireland for membership in the United Nations that nine members of the Security Council, on 13 September 1949, supported a draft resolution recommending the admission to the United Nations of Ireland, but that no recommendation was made to the General Assembly because of the opposition of one permanent member,

Deeming it important to the development of the United Nations that all applicant States which possess the qualifications for membership set forth in Article 4 of the Charter should be admitted,

Considering that the opposition to the application of Ireland was based on grounds not included in Article 4 of the Charter,

Recalling the recommendation of the General Assembly in resolution 197 (III) A of 8 December 1948 that each member of the Security Council and of the General Assembly, in exercising its vote on the admission of new Members, should act in accordance with the advisory opinion of the International Court of Justice of 28 May 1948, which declared that a State was not juridically entitled to make its consent to the admission dependent on conditions not expressly provided by paragraph 1 of Article 4,

1. *Reaffirms* its determination that Ireland is, in its judgment, a peace-loving State within the meaning of Article 4 of the Charter, is able and willing to carry out the obligations of the Charter, and should therefore be admitted to membership in the United Nations;

2. *Requests* the Security Council to reconsider the application of Ireland, in the light of this determination of the General Assembly.

252nd plenary meeting,
22 November 1949.

E

The General Assembly,

Noting from the special report[16] of the Security Council on the reconsideration of the application of Italy for membership in the United Nations that nine members of the Security Council, on 13 September 1949, supported a draft resolution recommending the admission to the United Nations of Italy, but that no recommendation was made to the General Assembly because of the opposition of one permanent member,

Deeming it important to the development of the United Nations that all applicant States which possess the qualifications for membership set forth in Article 4 of the Charter should be admitted,

Considering that the opposition to the application of Italy was based on grounds not included in Article 4 of the Charter,

Recalling the recommendation of the General Assembly in resolution 197 (III) A of 8 December 1948 that each member of the Security Council and of the General Assembly, in exercising its vote on the admission of new Members, should act in accordance with the advisory opinion of the International Court of Justice of 28 May 1948, which declared that a State was not juridically entitled to make its consent to the admission dependent on conditions not expressly provided by paragraph 1 of Article 4,

1. *Reaffirms* its determination that Italy is, in its judgment, a peace-loving State within the meaning of Article 4 of the Charter, is able and willing to carry out the obligations of the Charter, and should therefore be admitted to membership in the United Nations;

2. *Requests* the Security Council to reconsider the application of Italy, in the light of this determination of the General Assembly.

252nd plenary meeting,
22 November 1949.

---

[14] See *Official Records of the fourth session of the General Assembly, Annex to the Ad Hoc Political Committee,* document A/982.
[15] *Ibid.*
[16] *Ibid.*

19

F

The General Assembly,

Noting from the special report[17] of the Security Council on the reconsideration of the application of Jordan for membership in the United Nations that nine members of the Security Council, on 13 September 1949, supported a draft resolution recommending the admission to the United Nations of Jordan, but that no recommendation was made to the General Assembly because of the opposition of one permanent member,

Deeming it important to the development of the United Nations that all applicant States which possess the qualifications for membership set forth in Article 4 of the Charter should be admitted,

Considering that the opposition to the application of Jordan was based on grounds not included in Article 4 of the Charter,

Recalling the recommendation of the General Assembly in resolution 197 (III) A of 8 December 1948 that each member of the Security Council and of the General Assembly, in exercising its vote on the admission of new Members, should act in accordance with the advisory opinion of the International Court of Justice of 28 May 1948, which declared that a State was not juridically entitled to make its consent to the admission dependent on conditions not expressly provided by paragraph 1 of Article 4,

1. *Reaffirms* its determination that Jordan is, in its judgment, a peace-loving State within the meaning of Article 4 of the Charter, is able and willing to carry out the obligations of the Charter, and should therefore be admitted to membership in the United Nations;

2. *Requests* the Security Council to reconsider the application of Jordan, in the light of this determination of the General Assembly.

252nd plenary meeting,
22 November 1949.

G

The General Assembly,

Noting from the special report[18] of the Security Council that nine members of the Security Council, on 9 March 1949, supported a draft resolution recommending the admission to the United Nations of the Republic of Korea, but that no recommendation was made to the General Assembly because of the opposition of one permanent member,

Deeming it important to the development of the United Nations that all applicant States which possess the qualifications for membership set forth in Article 4 of the Charter should be admitted,

Considering that the opposition to the application of the Republic of Korea was based on grounds not included in Article 4 of the Charter,

Recalling the recommendation of the General Assembly in resolution 197 (III) A of 8 December 1948 that each member of the Security Council and of the General Assembly, in exercising its vote on the admission of new Members, should act in accordance with the advisory opinion of the International Court of Justice of 28 May 1948, which declared that a State was not juridically entitled to make its consent to the admission dependent on conditions not expressly provided by paragraph 1 of Article 4,

1. *Determines* that the Republic of Korea is, in its judgment, a peace-loving State within the meaning of Article 4 of the Charter, is able and willing to carry out the obligations of the Charter, and should therefore be admitted to membership in the United Nations;

2. *Requests* the Security Council to reconsider the application of the Republic of Korea, in the light of this determination of the General Assembly.

252nd plenary meeting,
22 November 1949.

H

The General Assembly,

Noting from the special report[19] of the Security Council on the reconsideration of the application of Portugal for membership in the United Nations that nine members of the Security Council, on 13 September 1949, supported a draft resolution recommending the admission to the United Nations of Portugal, but that no recommendation was made to the General Assembly because of the opposition of one permanent member,

Deeming it important to the development of the United Nations that all applicant States which possess the qualifications for membership set forth in Article 4 of the Charter should be admitted,

Considering that the opposition to the application of Portugal was based on grounds not included in Article 4 of the Charter,

Recalling the recommendation of the General Assembly in resolution 197 (III) A of 8 December 1948 that each member of the Security Council and of the General Assembly, in exercising its vote on the admission of new Members, should act in accordance with the advisory opinion of the International Court of Justice on 28 May 1948, which declared that a State was not juridically entitled to make its consent to the admission dependent on conditions not expressly provided by paragraph 1 of Article 4,

1. *Reaffirms* its determination that Portugal is, in its judgment, a peace-loving State within the meaning of Article 4 of the Charter, is able and willing to carry out the obligations of the Charter, and should therefore be admitted to membership in the United Nations;

2. *Requests* the Security Council to reconsider the application of Portugal, in the light of this determination of the General Assembly.

252nd plenary meeting,
22 November 1949.

---

[17] See *Official Records of the fourth session of the General Assembly, Annex to the Ad Hoc Political Committee,* document A/982.

[18] See *Official Records of the fourth session of the General Assembly, Annex to the Ad Hoc Political Committee,* document A/968.

[19] *Ibid.,* document A/982.

0014

I

The General Assembly,

Noting from the special report[20] of the Security Council that nine members of the Security Council, on 7 September 1949, supported a draft resolution recommending the admission to the United Nations of Nepal, but that no recommendation was made to the General Assembly because of the opposition of one permanent member,

Deeming it important to the development of the United Nations that all applicant States which possess the qualifications for membership set forth in Article 4 of the Charter should be admitted,

Considering that the opposition to the application of Nepal was based on grounds not included in Article 4 of the Charter,

Recalling the recommendation of the General Assembly in resolution 197 (III) A of 8 December 1948 that each member of the Security Council and of the General Assembly, in exercising its vote on the admission of new Members, should act in accordance with the advisory opinion of the International Court of Justice of 28 May 1948, which declared that a State was not juridically entitled to make its consent to the admission dependent on conditions not expressly provided by paragraph 1 of Article 4,

1. *Determines* that Nepal is, in its judgment, a peace-loving State within the meaning of Article 4 of the Charter, is able and willing to carry out the obligations of the Charter, and should therefore be admitted to membership in the United Nations;

2. *Requests* the Security Council to reconsider the application of Nepal, in the light of this determination of the General Assembly.

252nd plenary meeting,
22 November 1949.

J

The General Assembly,

Keeping in mind the discussion[21] concerning the admission of new Members in the *Ad Hoc* Political Committee at its fourth regular session,

Requests the International Court of Justice to give an advisory opinion on the following question:

"Can the admission of a State to membership in the United Nations, pursuant to Article 4, paragraph 2, of the Charter, be effected by a decision of the General Assembly when the Security Council has made no recommendation for admission by reason of the candidate failing to obtain the requisite majority or of the negative vote of a permanent member upon a resolution so to recommend?"

252nd plenary meeting,
22 November 1949.

---

[20] See *Official Records of the fourth session of the General Assembly, Annex to the Ad Hoc Political Committee,* document A/974.
[21] See *Official Records of the fourth session of the General Assembly, Ad Hoc* Political Committee, 25th-29th meetings inclusive.
[22] See *Official Records of the fourth session of the General Assembly, Annex to the Ad Hoc Political Committee,* document A/982.

K

The General Assembly,

Considering the special report[22] of the Security Council on the admission of new Members,

1. *Requests* the States permanent members of the Security Council to refrain from the use of the veto in connexion with the recommendation of States for membership in the United Nations;

2. *Requests* the Security Council to keep under consideration, in the light of Article 4, paragraph 1, of the Charter, the pending applications of all States which so far have not gained admission to the United Nations.

252nd plenary meeting,
22 November 1949.

297 (IV). United Nations Field Service and United Nations Panel of Field Observers

A

The General Assembly,

Having considered the report[23] of the Special Committee established by General Assembly resolution 270 (III)[24] of 29 April 1949,

Being of the opinion that the United Nations Field Service, as proposed by the Secretary-General in document A/AC.29/1[25] and modified by the report of the Special Committee, will contribute to the more efficient operation of United Nations missions,

Considering that the Secretary-General has authority to establish the United Nations Field Service, subject to budgetary limitations and the normal administrative controls of the General Assembly,

Takes note of the intention of the Secretary-General to establish this proposed unit as modified by the observations contained in the report of the Special Committee.

252nd plenary meeting,
22 November 1949.

B

The General Assembly,

Having considered the report of the Special Committee established by General Assembly resolution 270 (III) of 29 April 1949,

Desirous of facilitating the work of the United Nations in the pacific settlement of disputes under the provisions of the Charter,

Being of the opinion that the proposed United Nations Panel of Field Observers will contribute to this end,

Taking note of the intention of the Secretary-General to undertake the administrative arrangements for the proposed Panel with due regard to the observations contained in the report of the Special Committee,

---

[23] See *Official Records of the fourth session of the General Assembly,* Supplement No. 13.
[24] See *Official Records of the third session of the General Assembly, Part II,* Resolutions, page 16.
[25] See *Official Records of the fourth session of the General Assembly,* Supplement No. 13, annex I.

21

Noting that progress has been made by the present session of the General Assembly with regard to certain of the points contained in the memorandum of the Secretary-General,

Reaffirming its constant desire that all the resources of the United Nations Charter be utilized for the development of friendly relations between nations and the achievement of universal peace,

1. *Commends* the Secretary-General for his initiative in preparing his memorandum and presenting it to the General Assembly;

2. *Requests* the appropriate organs of the United Nations to give consideration to those portions of the memorandum of the Secretary-General with which they are particularly concerned;

3. *Requests* these organs to inform the General Assembly at its sixth session, through the Secretary-General, of any progress achieved through such consideration.

312th plenary meeting,
20 November 1950.

495 (V). Admission of new Members to the United Nations

The General Assembly,

Recalling its resolutions 296 (IV) A to I and K of 22 November 1949 concerning the reconsideration, by the Security Council, of pending applications for membership,

Noting that the General Assembly has not received recommendations for the admission of any of the applicants,

Requests the Security Council to keep the applications under consideration in accordance with the terms of the above-mentioned resolutions.

318th plenary meeting,
4 December 1950.

496 (V). International control of atomic energy

The General Assembly,

Recognizing that the effective regulation and reduction of national armaments would substantially diminish the present danger of war, relieve the heavy economic burden placed upon the peoples of the world in the absence of a system of armaments control, and permit the greater use of man's resources to projects devoted to his betterment,

Recognizing that the regulation and reduction of armaments to be effective must cover weapons of all kinds, must be based on unanimous agreement, and so must include every nation having substantial armaments and armed forces,

Recognizing further that any plan for the regulation and reduction of armaments and armed forces must be based upon safeguards that will secure the compliance of all nations,

Recognizing the inability to date to achieve agreement among nations on the elimination of atomic weapons under a system of effective international control of atomic energy and on the regulation and reduction of other armaments and armed forces,

Recalling that a plan[9] has been developed in the United Nations Atomic Energy Commission, and approved[10] by the General Assembly, for the international control of atomic energy, which would make effective the prohibition of atomic weapons; and that much useful planning work has been accomplished in the Commission for Conventional Armaments,

Desiring, however, to carry this work forward toward a comprehensive system of armaments control,

Decides to establish a committee of twelve, consisting of representatives of the members of the Security Council as of 1 January 1951, together with Canada, to consider and report to the next regular session of the General Assembly on ways and means whereby the work of the Atomic Energy Commission and the Commission for Conventional Armaments may be co-ordinated and on the advisability of their functions being merged and placed under a new and consolidated disarmament commission.

323rd plenary meeting,
13 December 1950.

497 (V). Place of meeting of the sixth regular session of the General Assembly

The General Assembly,

Considering that the building intended for the holding of the General Assembly will not be completed until 1952,

Considering that in these circumstances there may arise technical difficulties liable to impede the normal functioning of the General Assembly and the convenience of its deliberations,

1. *Decides*, in conformity with rule 3 of its rules of procedure, to convene its sixth regular session in Europe;

2. *Instructs* the President of the General Assembly and the Secretary-General to select the city most suitable for the above purpose and to make the necessary arrangements.

324th plenary meeting,
14 December 1950.

---

[9] See *Official Records of the Atomic Energy Commission, Special Supplement, Report to the Security Council*, Part II C and Part III; and *Ibid., Second Year, Special Supplement, Second Report to the Security Council*, Part II.

[10] See resolution 191 (III).

Printed in U.S.A. – 40897–February 1951–4,650
Reprinted in U.N., N.Y. – 07119–May 1968–200
May 1974–250

0016

Recalling in particular paragraph 6 of General Assembly resolution 917 (X) of 6 December 1955 calling upon the Government of the Union of South Africa to observe its obligations under the Charter of the United Nations,

Noting that resolution 616 B (VII) of 5 December 1952 declared, *inter alia*, that governmental policies which are designed to perpetuate or increase discrimination are inconsistent with the Charter,

Further noting that resolutions 395 (V) of 2 December 1950, 511 (VI) of 12 January 1952 and 616 A (VII) of 5 December 1952 have successively affirmed that a policy of "racial segregation" (*apartheid*) is necessarily based on doctrines of racial discrimination,

Convinced that, in a multi-racial society, harmony and respect for human rights and freedoms and the peaceful development of a unified community are best assured when patterns of legislation and practices are directed towards ensuring a legal order that will ensure equality before the law and the elimination of discrimination between all persons regardless of race, creed or colour,

Convinced also that a conciliatory approach in accordance with the principles of the Charter is necessary for progress towards a solution of this problem,

1. *Deplores* that the Government of the Union of South Africa has not yet observed its obligations under the Charter and has pressed forward with discriminatory measures which would make the future observance of those obligations more difficult;

2. *Affirms its conviction* that perseverance in such discriminatory policies is inconsistent not only with the Charter but with the forces of progress and international co-operation in implementing the ideals of equality, freedom and justice;

3. *Calls upon* the Government of the Union of South Africa to reconsider its position and revise its policies in the light of its obligations and responsibilities under the Charter and in the light of the principles subscribed to and the progress achieved in other contemporary multi-racial societies;

4. *Invites* the Government of the Union of South Africa to co-operate in a constructive approach to this question, more particularly by its presence in the United Nations;

5. *Requests* the Secretary-General, as appropriate, to communicate with the Government of the Union of South Africa to carry forward the purposes of the present resolution.

> *648th plenary meeting,*
> *30 January 1957.*

1017 (XI). Admission of new Members to the United Nations[5]

A

The General Assembly,

Recalling its resolution 296 G (IV) of 22 November 1949 finding the Republic of Korea qualified for membership in the United Nations,

Noting that the Republic of Korea has been excluded from membership in the United Nations because of the

opposition of one of the permanent members of the Security Council,

1. *Reaffirms its determination* that the Republic of Korea is fully qualified for admission to membership in the United Nations;

2. *Requests* the Security Council to reconsider the application of the Republic of Korea in the light of this determination and to report to the General Assembly as soon as possible.

> *663rd plenary meeting,*
> *28 February 1957.*

B

The General Assembly,

Recalling its resolution 620 C (VII) of 21 December 1952 finding Viet-Nam qualified for membership in the United Nations,

Noting that Viet-Nam has been excluded from membership in the United Nations because of the opposition of one of the permanent members of the Security Council,

1. *Reaffirms its determination* that Viet-Nam is fully qualified for admission to membership in the United Nations;

2. *Requests* the Security Council to reconsider the application of Viet-Nam in the light of this determination and to report to the General Assembly as soon as possible.

> *663rd plenary meeting,*
> *28 February 1957.*

1018 (XI). Report of the Director of the United Nations Relief and Works Agency for Palestine Refugees in the Near East

The General Assembly,

Recalling its resolutions 194 (III) of 11 December 1948, 302 (IV) of 8 December 1949, 393 (V) of 2 December 1950, 513 (VI) of 26 January 1952, 614 (VII) of 6 November 1952, 720 (VIII) of 27 November 1953, 818 (IX) of 4 December 1954 and 916 (X) of 3 December 1955,

Noting the annual report[6] and the special report[7] of the Director of the United Nations Relief and Works Agency for Palestine Refugees in the Near East and the report of the Advisory Commission of the Agency,[8]

Having reviewed the budget for relief and rehabilitation prepared by the Director of the Agency,

Noting with concern that contributions to that budget are not yet sufficient,

Noting that repatriation or compensation of the refugees, as provided for in paragraph 11 of resolution 194 (III), has not been effected, that no substantial progress has been made in the programme endorsed in paragraph 2 of resolution 513 (VI) for the reintegration of refugees and that, therefore, the situation of the refugees continues to be a matter of serious concern,

Noting that the host Governments have expressed the wish that the Agency continue to carry out its

---

[5] See also resolutions 1110 (XI), 1111 (XI), 1112 (XI), 1113 (XI) and 1118 (XI).

[6] *Official Records of the General Assembly, Eleventh Session,* Supplement No. 14, (A/3212).
[7] *Ibid., Supplement No. 14 A* (A/3212/Add.1).
[8] *Ibid., Eleventh Session, Annexes,* agenda item 23, document A/3498.

0017

RESOLUTIONS ADOPTED ON THE REPORTS OF THE SPECIAL POLITICAL COMMITTEE

CONTENTS

1144 (XII). Admission of new Members to the United Nations[1]

A

The General Assembly,

Recalling its resolutions 296 G (IV) of 22 November 1949 and 1017 A (XI) of 28 February 1957 finding the Republic of Korea qualified for membership in the United Nations,

Noting with regret the continued inability of the Security Council to recommend the admission of the Republic of Korea to membership in the United Nations owing to the negative vote of a permanent member of the Council,

Reaffirms that the Republic of Korea is fully qualified for and should be admitted to membership in the United Nations.

709th plenary meeting,
25 October 1957.

B

The General Assembly,

Recalling its resolutions 620 C (VII) of 21 December 1952 and 1017 B (XI) of 28 February 1957 finding Viet-Nam qualified for membership in the United Nations,

Noting with regret the continued inability of the Security Council to recommend the admission of Viet-Nam to membership in the United Nations owing to the negative vote of a permanent member of the Council,

Reaffirms that Viet-Nam is fully qualified for and should be admitted to membership in the United Nations.

709th plenary meeting,
25 October 1957.

1178 (XII). The question of race conflict in South Africa resulting from the policies of *apartheid* of the Government of the Union of South Africa

The General Assembly,

Recalling its previous resolutions, in particular resolutions 1016 (XI) of 30 January 1957, on the question of race conflict in South Africa resulting from the policies of *apartheid* of the Government of the Union of South Africa,

Recalling in particular paragraph 6 of its resolution 917 (X) of 6 December 1955, calling upon the Government of the Union of South Africa to observe its obligations under the Charter of the United Nations,

Noting that the General Assembly, in resolution 616 B (VII) of 5 December 1952, declared, *inter alia*, that governmental policies which are designed to perpetuate or increase discrimination are inconsistent with the Charter,

[1] See also resolution 1134 (XII).

7

0018

States. The second draft, in their opinion, opened the way to a speedy solution of the problem of the admission of new Members. The third draft, they argued, was contrary to the Charter, because it, *inter alia*, proposed the consideration at the seventh session of the Assembly of the question of appealing to the International Court of Justice for an advisory opinion on the voting procedure of the Security Council, a matter which lay outside the Court's jurisdiction.

The representative of Iraq declared that he would vote affirmatively for all three draft resolutions. The representative of Argentina said that he would abstain on draft resolutions one and three and would vote in favour of the second draft resolution.

The first draft resolution, originally sponsored by the representative of Peru, was adopted by 43 votes to 8, with 7 abstentions, at the 369th plenary meeting, as resolution 506 A (VI).

The Assembly, at its 370th plenary meeting on 1 February, decided, by 29 votes to 21, with 5 abstentions, that the adoption of the second draft resolution required a two-thirds majority of the Members present and voting. It then took a roll-call vote, the result being 22 votes in favour of the draft, 21 against, and 16 abstentions, as follows:

In favour: Afghanistan, Argentina, Burma, Byelorussian SSR, Czechoslovakia, Denmark, Egypt, Ethiopia, India, Indonesia, Iraq, Israel, Lebanon, Norway, Poland, Saudi Arabia, Sweden, Syria, Ukrainian SSR, USSR, Yemen, Yugoslavia.

Against: Bolivia, Brazil, China, Colombia, Costa Rica, Cuba, El Salvador, Greece, Haiti, Honduras, Luxembourg, Netherlands, Nicaragua, Panama, Paraguay, Peru, Philippines, Thailand, Turkey, United States, Venezuela.

Abstaining: Australia, Belgium, Canada, Chile, Dominican Republic, Ecuador, France, Guatemala, Iceland, Iran, Liberia, Mexico, New Zealand, Pakistan, United Kingdom, Uruguay.

The draft resolution was not adopted, as it failed to obtain the required two-thirds majority.

The third draft resolution was adopted at the 370th plenary meeting, by 36 votes to 5, with 14 abstentions, as resolution 506 B (VI).

The two resolutions adopted (506 A and B (VI)) read:

A

"*The General Assembly,*

"*Considering* that the Charter of the United Nations provides that membership is open to all States not original Members of the Organization and that this universality is subject only to the conditions that they be peace-loving and accept the obligations contained in the Charter and, in the judgment of the Organization, are able and willing to carry out these obligations,

"*Considering* that the judgment of the Organization that they are willing and able to carry out these obligations and are otherwise qualified for membership ought to be based on facts such as: the maintenance of friendly relations with other States, the fulfilment of international obligations and the record of a State's willingness and present disposition to submit international claims or controversies to pacific means of settlement established by international law,

"*Considering* that, according to the advisory opinion of the International Court of Justice of 28 May 1948, a Member of the United Nations voting on the application of a State for membership in the United Nations is not juridically entitled to make its consent to admission dependent on conditions not expressly provided by paragraph 1 of Article 4 of the Charter; and that this opinion excludes the possibility that, consistently with the letter and spirit of the Charter, Members can base their votes on motives which are outside the scope of Article 4 of the Charter,

"*Considering* that, not only for these reasons but also according to principles of international justice, it is not possible to deny to States candidates for membership in the United Nations the right to present proofs on facts such as those recited in the first paragraph of the preamble,

"*Recalling and reaffirming* General Assembly resolutions 197 B (III) of 8 December 1948 and 296 K (IV) of 22 November 1949,

"1. *Declares* that the judgment of the United Nations on the admission of new Members ought to be based exclusively on the conditions contained in Article 4 of the Charter;

"2. *Recommends* that the Security Council reconsider all pending applications for the admission of new Members; that in this reconsideration, as well as in the consideration of all future applications, the members of the Council take into account such facts and evidence as States applicants for membership may present; and that the Security Council base its action exclusively on the conditions contained in the Charter and on the facts establishing the existence of these conditions;

"3. *Requests* the permanent members of the Security Council to confer with one another soon with a view to assisting the Council to come to positive recommendations in regard to the pending applications for membership."

B

"*The General Assembly,*

"*Having regard* to the importance of the admission of new Members from the point of view of the achievement of the purposes of the United Nations,

"*Desiring* that the draft resolution submitted by the delegations of Costa Rica, El Salvador, Guatemala, Honduras and Nicaragua [A/C.1/708] requesting the International Court of Justice to give a further advisory opinion on the matter should be fully considered in all its aspects,

"*Decides*

"1. To request the Security Council to report to the General Assembly at its seventh session on the status of applications still pending;

0019

"2. To direct that the item "Admission of new Members" shall be included in the provisional agenda of the General Assembly at its next regular session;

"3. To refer the draft resolution submitted by the delegations mentioned above and contained in document A/C.1/708 to the General Assembly at its next regular session for consideration under that item."

2. Consideration by the Security Council

On 10 December 1951, the Secretary-General transmitted (S/2435) to the Security Council the text of resolution 550(VI)[19] on the question of the full participation of Italy in the work of the Trusteeship Council, adopted by the Assembly on 7 December 1951. This recommended that the Council give urgent consideration to the resolution with a view to recommending the immediate admission of Italy to membership in the United Nations.

The Security Council considered the question at its 568th, 569th and 573rd meetings held on 18 and 19 December 1951 and 6 February 1952.

The provisional agenda of the Security Council's 568th meeting on 18 December consisted of: (1) adoption of the agenda; (2) the Secretary-General's letter (S/2435) transmitting the text of Assembly resolution 550(VI) concerning the admission of Italy; and (3) a letter from the Secretary-General (S/1936), dated 6 December 1950, transmitting the text of Assembly resolution 495(V)[20], adopted on 4 December 1950 concerning the admission of new Members.

The President of the Council stated that the order of the provisional agenda was due to the urgent nature of resolution 550(VI); resolution 490(V) made no mention of urgency.

The representative of the USSR considered that items 2 and 3 of the provisional agenda should be reversed and submitted a formal, oral motion to that effect. Resolution 495(V) had been adopted a year earlier than resolution 550(VI) and should therefore be dealt with first. He pointed out that if the Council dealt with item 3 first, it would also be referring to a question included in item 2, namely, the admission of Italy to membership in the United Nations.

Further, if the Council considered item 3 first and decided to admit all the thirteen States which had submitted applications for admission to the United Nations, that is, Albania, Austria, Bulgaria, Ceylon, Finland, Hungary, Ireland, Italy, Jordan, the Mongolian People's Republic, Nepal, Portugal and Romania, then it would solve more rapidly the problem of the admission of Italy. In that way

both urgency and justice would be respected. But if the Council considered the question of the admission of Italy first, reached no agreement, and took no decision, the matter would not have been expedited at all. The whole problem of the admission of new Members to the United Nations was a very important one, he said, although owing to the policy of discrimination and favouritism practised by the United States, with the support of the United Kingdom, it had not so far been solved. The fact that Italy was the Administering Authority for a Trust Territory did not mean that some special priority had to be given to the study of its admission to membership, he maintained.

The representatives of Brazil, China, Ecuador, France, the Netherlands, Turkey, the United Kingdom and the United States opposed the USSR proposal to consider item 3 of the provisional agenda first. They argued that the special question of Italy ought to be given priority over the general question of the admission of new Members. The admission of Italy to membership in the United Nations was submitted by the General Assembly as an urgent question. Italy, they said, was a special case since the United Nations had charged it with special responsibilities as the Administering Authority of Somaliland. They felt, in general, that Italy could not execute its duties completely and fully without having all the rights of a Member of the United Nations. Item 3, they said, having been left unconsidered for over a year, could not now become so urgent that it should be given priority over item 2. It was pointed out that resolution 495(V) referred not to all pending thirteen applications for membership in the United Nations, but only to nine and that, even there, the only request which had been made to the Council had been that it should keep those nine applications under consideration. It was further argued that the application of one single State should not be related to the applications of other States. In reply to the representative of the USSR, the representative of the United States declared that his Government warmly supported the admission of applicants which met the requirements of Article 4 of the Charter.

The representatives of India and Yugoslavia stated that the admission of Italy was, undoubtedly, a matter of urgency, but that was not to say that the admission of other applicants was not

---

[19] See p. 92.
[20] See *Y.U.N., 1950*, p. 413.

아국의 유엔가입 촉구 총회결의안 추진 문제

1990. 4.

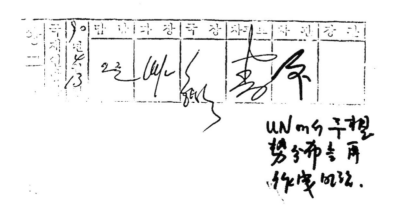

UN가입 구체
勢力布告 再
檢討 必要.

0021

我國의 유엔加入 促求 總會決議案 推進 問題

1990. 4.

0022

- 目 次 -

I. 問題의 提起

II. 總會決議案 推進問題 檢討

III. 北韓側의 豫想反應

Ⅰ. 問題의 提起

○ 아국 外交政策의 숙원과제인 유엔加入은 유엔 安全保障理事會
  에서 拒否權을 가지고 있는 常任理事國中 소련과 중국의 否定
  的인 態度로 實現되지 못하고 있음.

○ 최근 國際社會의 전반적인 平和, 協力雰圍氣와 아국의 國際的
  位相 浮刻 및 北方政策을 통한 東歐圈과의 關係改善으로 유엔
  加入 實現을 위한 분위기는 과거 어느때보다 改善되었으나,
  소·중, 특히 중국의 拒否權 行使 可能性은 尙存하며, 이들
  國家의 肯定的 態度 變化가 확인되지 않은 상황에서 我國의
  유엔加入 實現은 사실상 어려운 상태임.

○ 따라서, 소·중에 대하여 我國加入問題에 拒否權을 行使하지
  않도록 說得하는 것이 현시점에서 我國 유엔加入 實現의 관건
  이라고 할 수 있음.

○ 이같은 상황에서, 多数決의 原則이 適用되는 유엔總會에
  아국의 유엔가입을 촉구하는 決議案을 提出하는 문제에
  관하여 그 長短點 및 關聯事項을 檢討코자 함.

0024

Ⅱ. 總會 決議案 推進問題 檢討

1. 肯定的인 側面

° 我國 유엔加入 支持 基盤 確認
 - 多数 유엔會員國의 찬성으로 決議를 採擇시켜 國際
   社會에서의 아국 유엔가입에 대한 支持基盤을 確認하고,
   支持규모의 勢誇示가 가능함.

° 소.중의 拒否權 不在 및 不參等 投票態度 變化期待 가능
 - 安保理와는 달리 소.중이 反對하더라도 決議案을 採擇
   시킬 수 있음.
 - 동 總會決議案 採擇으로 아국의 유엔加入이 實現되는
   것이 아니므로 소.중, 특히 蘇聯은 棄權, 投票不參등
   으로 적극적 反對는 表明하지 않을 가능성이 있음.

° 我國 유엔加入 實現 분위기 고조
 - 壓倒的 多数로 採擇될시 아국 유엔가입의 당위성이
   國際社會에서 뚜렷이 浮刻됨으로써 아국加入 促求
   與論을 환기시킬 수 있음.
 - 소.중에 대하여 추후 拒否權 行使를 自制하도록 하는
   國際的인 壓力으로 作用할 수 있음.

2. 否定的 側面

ㅇ 유엔에서의 南北韓 對決 再燃

  - 北韓의 强力한 反對 策動이 예상되며, 이로 인하여
    유엔에서 南北韓間의 對決이 不可避함.
    (Ⅲ항 북한 예상반응 참조)

  - 이는 유엔에서 韓國問題 討議 지양을 밝혀온 우리의
    입장 및 특히 7.7 宣言이후 我國의 和解指向 政策과
    矛盾됨.

ㅇ 大多数 贊成票 確保를 위한 外交的 負擔

  - 단순한 決議의 採擇만으로는 아국유엔가입 支持 基盤
    確認의 의미가 적으므로, 절대 다수국가의 贊成確保를
    위한 外交的 負擔이 높음.
    (결의안 채택시에도 다수가 기권하고 단순히 찬성이
     반대보다 많은 경우 意味 別無)
    * 決議案 採擇에는 投票國家中 棄權을 除外하고 2/3
      贊成 필요

  - 아국의 유엔加入 問題는 戰後 冷戰의 유물로 認識되고
    있으며 많은 會員國들이 事案 자체보다는 關係强大國
    들의 態度를 意識하여 투표에 임하는 성향이 있음.

ㅇ 總會決議 자체가 아국 유엔加入 實現과는 직접적으로 無關

  - 아국의 유엔加入問題를 安保理에서 再審하여 줄것을
    促求하는 内容의 유엔總會決議는 안보리에 대한 구속적
    효과가 없으므로 加入實現과 直接 連繫되지 않음.

0026

o 北方外交에 대한 否定的 影響 가능

- 我國加入 實現에 관건이 되는 대소.중 설득을 위해 總會
  決議案 探擇과 같은 공개적 압력이 外交的으로 바람직
  스러울지 신중한 檢討가 要望됨.

o 節次的 問題

- 總會 決議案 推進을 위하여는 關聯議題가 있어야 할
  것인 바, 我國加入 促求 決議案은 과거 事例(별첨 관련
  절차 참고)와 같이 "신규회원국의 가입(Admission of
  New Members)" 의제하에 提出할 수 있을 것임.
- 我國 加入問題가 1949년이래 安保理에 未決 案件으로
  되어 있고, 그간 4차례에 걸쳐 我國加入 관련 總會
  決議가 探擇된 바 있으므로, 동 총회결의안 추진에
  節次的인 하자는 없을 것임.
- 다만, 新規會員國의 加入問題의 1차적 管轄權을
  安保理가 가지고 있는데 비추어, 일부에서는 總會
  決議案 審議에 앞서 安保理의 再審議가 있어야 한다는
  논란이 있을 可能性도 있음.

3. 結 論

o 상기와 같은 長短點을 고려할때, 我國 유엔加入 促求
  總會 決議案 推進은 신중한 檢討가 필요함.

o 동 추진문제는 유엔 核心友邦國 協議會 제 2차회의
  (5월초 개최 예정)시에도 討議 豫定이므로, 동 會議 結果와
  추후 關聯國際狀況의 進展을 계속 檢討한후 立場을 定立
  함이 좋을 것으로 사료됨.

0027

Ⅲ. 北韓側의 豫想 反應

1. 對應 決議案 提出

o 新規會員國 加入 議題하에서 南北韓의 統一後 加入 또는
  單一 國號下의 加入을 촉구하는 決議案 提出 가능

o 韓半島 問題를 부활시키는 새로운 議題(예 : 1975년
  한국문제 관련 결의의 이행)를 상정, 對應 決議案 提出
  가능

o 아측 決議案 內容을 稀釋시켜, 효과면에서 무의미하게
  만드는 修正案 推進 가능

o 南北韓 決議案을 모두 撤回토록 誘導 努力 가능

2. 我側 決議案 否決 策動

o 我側決議案을 否決시키기 위하여 유엔 會員國들의 反對
  또는 棄權 誘導 노력

o 非同盟 過激勢力等 北韓 同調國家 總動員 예상

0028

Ⅰ. 관련 검토사항

1. 과거 사례

49.4.8.   안보리, 아국가입 권고결의안 부결(소련 거부권행사)

<u>49.11.22.</u> 총회, 한국가입신청 재심의를 안보리에 요청하는
            결의 채택 〈결의 296 G(Ⅳ)〉

<u>50.12.4.</u>   총회, 한국포함 9개국 가입신청의 계속 검토를
            안보리에 요청하는 결의 채택 〈결의 495 (Ⅴ)〉

'55.12.8.   총회, 18개국 가입권고 공동결의안 채택

            〈결의 918(Ⅹ)〉

            * 쿠바는, 한국, 베트남을 포함한 수정결의안을
              제출했다가 철회

<u>57.2.28.</u>   총회, 한국가입신청 재심의를 안보리에 요청하는
            결의 채택 〈결의 1017 A(ⅩⅡ)〉

57.9.9.   안보리, 한국가입에 관한 8개국 공동결의안 부결
            (소련 거부권행사)

<u>57.10.25.</u> 총회, 한국의 유엔가입 타당성 재확인 결의 채택
            〈결의 1144 A(ⅩⅡ)〉

0029

58.12.9.   안보리, 한국가입에 관한 4개국 공동견의안 부결
            (소련 거부권행사)

75.8.6.   안보리, 한국가입신청 의제 채택 부결(7:6:2)

75.9.26.   안보리, 한국가입신청 의제 채택 부결(7:7:1)

2. 추진시 관련 절차

   가. 총회의제 문제

       ○ 과거 아국유엔가입 촉구 총회 결의안(4회)은 모두
         "신규회원국의 가입(Admssion of New Members)"
         의제하에 제출, 채택되었음. (특정위 심의후 본회의
         심의)

       ○ 따라서 결의안을 제출코자 할 경우 총회에 매년 자동적
         으로 상정되는 신규회원가입 의제하에 우방국들이 "한국
         가입이 안보리의 권고안 채택 실패로 부결되어온 부당성을
         지적하고, 한국가입 실현을 위한 안보리의 행동을 촉구
         하는 "내용의 결의안을 제출하는 방식으로 추진할 수
         있을 것임.

       * 다만, 금후 추진 결정시에는 유엔 사무국에 본 절차문제
         확인 필요

0030

나. 의결 정족수 문제

   ο 동 결의안은 신규회원국 가입 의제하에 제출케 될
      것이므로, 투표국가중 기권을 제외하고 2/3 찬성 필요
      (여타 의제하에 추진하더라도 국제평화와 안보관련
      문제는 2/3 찬성 필요)

0031

기 안 용 지

분류기호 문서번호	국연 2031-	(전화 :)		시 행 상 특별취급	
보존기간	영구·준영구. 10. 5. 3. 1.	장 관			
수 신 처 보존기간		송OOT			
시행일자	1990. 4. 18.				

보조기관	국 장	전결	협조기관		문 서 통 제	접 열 1990.4.18
	과 장				발 송 인	1990.4.18
기안책임자	오 준					

경 유			발신명의	
수 신	주유연 대사			
참 조				

제 목	검토서 송부

1. 아국 유연가입을 촉구하는 내용의 유연총회 결의안 채택

문제에 관한 본부의 검토서를 별첨 송부하니 참고하시기 바랍니다.

2. 5월 개최예정인 CG 2차회의시 동 회의결 의안 추진

문제가 검토될 수 있도록 CG 참석국들에게 사전 협의 바랍니다.

바랍니다.

첨 부 : 동 검토서 1부. 끝.

이미 file 되어
있으니 폐기
유엔가입(아국입장)

我國의 유엔加入 促求 總會決議案 推進 問題

1990. 4.

0033

- 目 次 -

I. 問題의 提起

II. 總會決議案 推進問題 檢討

III. 北韓側의 豫想反應

첨 부 : 1. 關聯 檢討事項

2. 88年 我國代表 總會演說 推進時 票勢 最終分析

3. 過去 我國加入 促求 總會決議 寫本 (4건)

0034

Ⅰ. 問題의 提起

o 아국 外交政策의 숙원과제인 유엔加入은 유엔 安全保障理事會
  에서 拒否權을 가지고 있는 常任理事國中 소련과 중국의 否定
  的인 態度로 實現되지 못하고 있음.

o 최근 國際社會의 전반적인 平和, 協力雰圍氣와 아국의 國際的
  位相 浮刻 및 北方政策을 통한 東歐圈과의 關係改善으로 유엔
  加入 實現을 위한 분위기는 과거 어느때보다 改善되었으나,
  소.중, 특히 중국의 拒否權 行使 可能性은 尙存하며, 이들
  國家의 肯定的 態度 變化가 확인되지 않은 상황에서 我國의
  유엔加入 實現은 사실상 어려운 상태임.

o 따라서, 소.중에 대하여 我國加入問題에 拒否權을 行使하지
  않도록 說得하는 것이 현시점에서 我國 유엔加入 實現의 관건
  이라고 할 수 있음.

o 이같은 상황에서, 多數決의 原則이 適用되는 유엔總會에
  아국의 유엔가입을 촉구하는 決議案을 提出하는 문제에
  관하여 그 長短點 및 關聯事項을 檢討코자 함.

0035

Ⅱ. 總會 決議案 推進問題 檢討

1. 肯定的인 側面

○ 我國 유엔加入 支持 基盤 確認

- 多數 유엔會員國의 찬성으로 決議를 採擇시켜 國際
  社會에서의 아국 유엔가입에 대한 支持基盤을 確認하고,
  支持규모의 勢誇示가 가능함.

○ 소.중의 拒否權 不在 및 不參等 投票態度 變化期待 가능

- 安保理와는 달리 소.중이 反對하더라도 決議案을 採擇
  시킬 수 있음.

- 동 總會決議案 採擇으로 아국의 유엔加入이 實現되는
  것이 아니므로 소.중, 특히 蘇聯은 棄權, 投票不參등
  으로 적극적 反對는 表明하지 않을 가능성이 있음.

○ 我國 유엔加入 實現 분위기 고조

- 壓倒的 多數로 採擇될시 아국 유엔가입의 당위성이
  國際社會에서 뚜렷이 浮刻됨으로써 아국加入 促求
  與論을 환기시킬 수 있음.

- 소.중에 대하여 추후 拒否權 行使를 自制하도록 하는
  國際的인 壓力으로 作用할 수 있음.

0036

2. 否定的 側面

　o　유엔에서의 南北韓 對決 再燃

　　－ 北韓의 强力한 反對 策動이 예상되며, 이로 인하여
　　　유엔에서 南北韓間의 對決이 不可避함.
　　　(Ⅲ항 북한 예상반응 참조)

　　－ 이는 유엔에서 韓國問題 討議 지양을 밝혀온 우리의
　　　입장 및 특히 7.7 宣言이후 我國의 和解指向 政策과
　　　矛盾됨.

　o　大多數 贊成票 確保를 위한 外交的 負擔

　　－ 단순한 決議의 採擇만으로는 아국유엔가입 支持 基盤
　　　確認의 의미가 적으므로, 절대 다수국가의 贊成確保를
　　　위한 外交的 負擔이 높음.
　　　(결의안 채택시에도 다수가 기권하고 단순히 찬성이
　　　　반대보다 많은 경우 意味 別無)

　　　＊ 決議案 採擇에는 投票國家中 棄權을 除外하고 2/3
　　　　 贊成 필요

　　－ 아국의 유엔加入 問題는 戰後 冷戰의 유물로 認識되고
　　　있으며 많은 會員國들이 事案 자체보다는 關係强大國
　　　들의 態度를 意識하여 투표에 임하는 성향이 있음.

　o　總會決議 자체가 아국 유엔加入 實現과는 직접적으로 無關

　　－ 아국의 유엔加入問題를 安保理에서 再審하여 줄것을
　　　促求하는 內容의 유엔總會決議는 안보리에 대한 구속적
　　　효과가 없으므로 加入實現과 直接 連繫되지 않음.

0037

o 北方外交에 대한 否定的 影響 가능

- 我國加入 實現에 관건이 되는 대소.중 설득을 위해 總會
  決議案 採擇과 같은 공개적 압력이 外交的으로 바람직
  스러울지 신중한 檢討가 要望됨.

o 節次的 問題

- 總會 決議案 推進을 위하여는 關聯議題가 있어야 할
  것인 바, 我國加入 促求 決議案은 과거 事例(별첨 관련
  절차 참고)와 같이 "신규회원국의 가입(Admission of
  New Members)" 의제하에 提出할 수 있을 것임.

- 我國 加入問題가 1949년이래 安保理에 未決 案件으로
  되어 있고, 그간 4차례에 걸쳐 我國加入 관련 總會
  決議가 採擇된 바 있으므로, 동 총회결의안 추진에
  節次的인 하자는 없을 것임.

- 다만, 新規會員國의 加入問題의 1차적 管轄權을
  安保理가 가지고 있는데 비추어, 일부에서는 總會
  決議案 審議에 앞서 安保理의 再審議가 있어야 한다는
  논란이 있을 可能性도 있음.

3. 結 論

o 상기와 같은 長短點을 고려할때, 我國 유엔加入 促求
  總會 決議案 推進은 신중한 檢討가 필요함.

o 동 추진문제는 유엔 核心友邦國 協議會 제 2차회의
  (5월초 개최 예정)시에도 討議 豫定이므로, 동 會議 結果와
  추후 關聯國際狀況의 進展을 계속 檢討한후 立場을 定立
  함이 좋을 것으로 사료됨.

0038

Ⅲ. 北韓側의 豫想 反應

1. 對應 決議案 提出

ㅇ 新規會員國 加入 議題下에서 南北韓의 統一後 加入 또는
單一 國號下의 加入을 촉구하는 決議案 提出 가능

ㅇ 韓半島 問題를 부활시키는 새로운 議題(예 : 1975년
한국문제 관련 결의의 이행)를 상정, 對應 決議案 提出
가능

ㅇ 아측 決議案 內容을 稀釋시켜, 효과면에서 무의미하게
만드는 修正案 推進 가능

ㅇ 南北韓 決議案을 모두 撤回토록 誘導 努力 가능

2. 我側 決議案 否決 策動

ㅇ 我側決議案을 否決시키기 위하여 유엔 會員國들의 反對
또는 棄權 誘導 노력

ㅇ 非同盟 過激勢力等 北韓 同調國家 總動員 예상

0039

(첨부 1)

Ⅰ. 관련 검토사항

1. 과거 사례

49.4.8.   안보리, 아국가입 권고결의안 부결(소련 거부권행사)

49.11.22.   총회, 한국가입신청 재심의를 안보리에 요청하는
            결의 채택 〈결의 296 G(Ⅳ)〉

50.12.4.   총회, 한국포함 9개국 가입신청의 계속 검토를
            안보리에 요청하는 결의 채택 〈결의 495 (Ⅴ)〉

55.12.8.   총회, 18개국 가입권고 공동결의안 채택

            〈결의 918(X)〉
            * 쿠바는, 한국, 베트남을 포함한 수정결의안을
              제출했다가 철회

57.2.28.   총회, 한국가입신청 재심의를 안보리에 요청하는
            결의 채택 〈결의 1017 A(XII)〉

57.9.9.   안보리, 한국가입에 관한 8개국 공동결의안 부결
            (소련 거부권행사)

57.10.25.   총회, 한국의 유엔가입 타당성 재확인 결의 채택
            〈결의 1144 A(XII)〉

0040

58.12.9.　　안보리, 한국가입에 관한 4개국 공동결의안 부결
　　　　　　　　（소련 거부권행사）

75.8.6.　　　안보리, 한국가입신청 의제 채택 부결(7:6:2)

75.9.26.　　안보리, 한국가입신청 의제 채택 부결(7:7:1)

2. 추진시 관련 절차

　가. 총회의제 문제

　　　o 과거 아국유엔가입 촉구 총회 결의안(4회)은 모두
　　　　"신규회원국의 가입(Admssion of New Members)"
　　　　의제하에 제출, 채택되었음. (특정위 심의후 본회의
　　　　심의)

　　　o 따라서 결의안을 제출코자 할 경우 총회에 매년 자동적
　　　　으로 상정되는 신규회원가입 의제하에 우방국들이 "한국
　　　　가입이 안보리의 권고안 채택 실패로 부결되어온 부당성을
　　　　지적하고, 한국가입 실현을 위한 안보리의 행동을 촉구
　　　　하는 "내용의 결의안을 제출하는 방식으로 추진할 수
　　　　있을 것임.

　　　* 다만, 금후 추진 결정시에는 유엔 사무국에 본 절차문제
　　　　확인 필요

0041

나. 의결 정족수 문제

    ㅇ 동 결의안은 신규회원국 가입 의제하에 제출케 될
       것이므로, 투표국가중 기권을 제외하고 2/3 찬성 필요
       (여타 의제하에 추진하더라도 국제평화와 안보관련
       문제는 2/3 찬성 필요)

0042

보편성 원칙에 관한 유엔총회 결의안(안)

The General Assembly,

Noting with satisfaction the recent improved international atmosphere and the trend to strengthen the role of the United Nations in resolving regional conflicts and promoting international peace and cooperation,

Bearing in mind that the role of the United Nations can best be enhanced when all States participate in the work of the Organization in conformity with the principle of universality,

Further noting that, notwithstanding the final achievement of the decolonization process, the goal of universal membership in the United Nations has not yet been fully attained,

Convinced that the principle of universality implies that all States qualified for membership according to Article 4 of the Charter and willing to join should be admitted to the Organization,

[Considering in particular that United Nations membership of divided nations does not prejudice either their efforts for reunification or an eventual single membership after their reunification,]

1. Declares that the judgment of the United Nations on the admission of new Members ought to be based exclusively on the conditions contained in Article 4 of the Charter,

2. Calls upon the Security Council to review, as a matter of priority, the question of universal membership in the United Nations, taking into account the still unresolved requests for admission by States willing to become member of the Organization, and to recommend further action by the General Assembly,

3. Requests the permanent members of the Security Council to confer with one another soon with a view to assisting the Council to come to positive recommendations in regard to the pending applications for membership.

0043

(DRAFT RESOLUTION III)

The General Assembly,

Noting with satisfaction the recent improved international atmosphere and the trend to strengthen the role of the United Nations in resolving regional conflicts and promoting international peace and security,

[Commending the Secretary-General for his preeminent role in bringing about negotiated solutions of regional conflicts through his good-offices and mediation,]

Bearing in mind that the role of the United Nations can best be enhanced when all States participate in the work of the Organization in conformity with the principle of universality,

Further noting that, notwithstanding the final achievement of the decolonization process, the goal of universal membership in the United Nations has not yet been fully attained,

Convinced that the principle of universality implies that all States qualified for membership according to Article 4 of the Charter and willing to join should be admitted to the Organization,

Calls upon the Security Council to review, as a matter of priority, the question of universal membership in the United Nations, taking into account the still unresolved requests for admission by States willing to become member of the Organization, and to recommend further action by the General Assembly.

0044

(DRAFT RESOLUTION)

The General Assembly,

Noting with satisfaction the recent trend in the inter-national community to strengthen the role of the United Nations in helping to resolve regional conflicts and promoting reconciliation and cooperation,

Reaffirming its resolutions 296 G(IV) of 22 November 1949 and 1017A (XI) of 28 February 1957 finding the Republic of Korea fully qualified for admission to membership in the United Nations,

Convinced that all applicant States which possess the qualifications for membership set for in Article 4 of the Charter should be admitted without delay in confirmity with the principle of universality,

Noting with regret that the Republic of Korea is the only remaining State which has been denied its membership in the United Nations for the last four decades against its will and despite its qualification on grounds not provided in Article 4 of the Charter,

Considering that the admission of the Republic of Korea at this juncture, reflecting the recent improvement of international atmosphere involving the Korean peninsula, would not only enable the Republic of Korea to contribute to international peace and cooperation, but also reduce tension in the area and facilitate the process of inter-Korean reconciliation toward the goal of reunification,

either Further considering that the admission of the Republic of Korea, as an interim measure pending reunification of Korea, does not prejudice the right of the Democratic People's Republic of Korea to apply for separate membership, if and whenever it so wishes, or an eventual single membership in the United Nations after the reunification of the country,

Requests the Security Council to reconsider the application of the Republic of Korea for membership in the United Nations and to report to the General Assembly as soon as possible;

Calls upon the two Korean Governments to accelerate their dialogue and negotiation for reconciliation and reunification;

Invites the Governments concerned to cooperate closely among themselves and with the two Korean Governments in order to create in and around the Korean peninsula conditions conducive to normalization of relations, peace and stability in the region, and to peaceful reunification of Korea.

0045

(DRAFT RESOLUTION I)

The General Assembly,

Noting with satisfaction the recent trend in the international community to strengthen the role of the United Nations
in helping to resolve regional conflicts and promoting reconciliation and cooperation,

Reaffirming its resolutions 296 G(IV) of 22 November 1949
and 1017A (XI) of 28 February 1957 finding the Republic of Korea
fully qualified for admission to membership in the United Nations,

Convinced that all the applicant States which possess the
qualifications for membership set forth in Article 4 of the Charter
should be admitted without delay in conformity with the principle
of universality,

Noting with regret that the Republic of Korea is the only
remaining State which has been denied its membership in the United
Nations for the last four decades against its will and despite its
qualification on grounds not set forth in Article 4 of the Charter,

Considering that the admission of the Republic of Korea at
this juncture, reflecting the recent improvement of the international
atmosphere surrounding the Korean peninsula, would not only enable
the Republic of Korea to contribute to international peace and
cooperation, but also reduce tension in the area and facilitate
the process of inter-Korean reconciliation toward the goal of
reunification,

Further considering that the admission of the Republic of
Korea, as an interim measure pending the reunification of Korea,
does not prejudice either the right of the Democratic People's
Republic of Korea to apply for separate membership, if and whenever
it so wishes, or an eventual single membership in the United Nations
after the reunification of the country,

Requests the Security Council to reconsider the application
of the Republic of Korea for membership in the United Nations and
to submit its report thereon to the General Assembly as soon as
possible;

Calls upon the two Korean Governments to accelerate their
dialogue and negotiations for reconciliation and reunification;

Invites the Governments concerned to cooperate closely among
themselves and with the two Korean Governments in order to create
in and around the Korean peninsula conditions conducive to the
normalization of relations, peace and stability in the region, and
peaceful reunification of Korea.

0046

(DRAFT RESOLUTION)

   The General Assembly,

   Noting with satisfaction the recent trend under the
improved international atmosphere to strengthen the role
of the United Nations in helping resolve regional conflicts
and promoting international peace and security,

   Bearing in mind that the role of the United Nations
can best be enhanced when all States participate in the work
of the Organization in conformity with the principle of
universality,

   Further noting that, notwithstanding the final achievement of the decolonization process, the goal of universality
of membership in the United Nations has not been fully attained,

   Convinced that all States qualified for membership
according to Article 4 of the Charter and willing to join the
Organization should be admitted in conformity with the principle
of universality,

   Calls upon the Security Council to review, as a
matter of priority, the question of universal membership
in the United Nations, taking into account the still unsolved
requests for admission, and to make recommendation thereon to
the General Assembly;

   [Requests the Secretary-General to provide his good-
offices to facilitate the process of consultation among the
parties directly concerned towards agreement on universal
membership;]

   Expresses the hope that universality of membership in
the United Nations will be fully realized as soon as possible
through the admission of the remaining non-member States
desiring to join the Organization.

0047

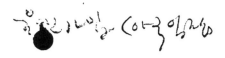

Eric Suy 교수의 견해 요지

(기본입장)

ㅇ 궁극적으로 한국의 유엔가입 실현을 위하여는 거부권의 행사가
   예상되는 안보리에서 당장 추진할 것이 아니라 먼저 총회에서
   한국문제를 하나의 의제로 토론케 하는 것이 바람직함.

ㅇ 그러나 토론후 추진될 결의안은 가입문제에 국한하거나 또는
   전반적인 남북한 문제를 다루는 것이 아니라, 양자를 적절히 절충
   하여 유엔사무총장으로 하여금 한반도 문제에 관하여 중재(Good
   Office)를 하도록 요청하는 내용이 되는 것이 좋을 것임.

ㅇ 사무총장은 본문제 해결에 적극적인 자세를 가지고 다음번 해결
   해야 할 주요 분쟁으로 인식하고 있을 것으로 사료되는 바, 그로
   하여금 점진적으로 한국문제 해결을 도모케 할 경우 궁극적으로
   가입문제도 해결될 수 있을 것임.

(상기 경우 유엔에서의 한반도문제 재연 불가피 가능성에 대하여)

ㅇ 추진 결의안 내용에 달려있는 바, 사전에 한국문제 전반을 토의
   하자는 것이 아님을 분명히 하고 사무총장의 중재를 요청하는
   내용으로 할 경우 과거 사안의 재탕이라고는 안볼 것임.

0048

(안보리에 문제제기 또는 총회에 직접 제기하는 경우)

o 소련의 태도 변화 가능 불구, 중국측의 거부권 행사가 확실한
   상황에서 안보리에 가입 신청은 바람직 하지 않음.

o 가입문제만을 안보리에서의 토의없이 막바로 총회에 제기하는 것은
   최소 북한의 확고한 지지국들이 가입문제에 1차적 관할권을 가진
   안보리에서의 토의없이 권한없는 총회에 제기하는 것은 부적합하다는
   절차적, 법적 문제점을 거론할 가능성이 큼.

o 따라서 보편성원칙등 가입문제에 관한 문구가 포함되고, 한반도
   문제해결을 위한 유엔사무총장의 역할을 요청하는 내용의 결의안을
   총회에 내보는 방안을 검토할 수 있을 것임.

(평   가)

o 남북한이 "문제의 당사자 해결 원칙"을 주장하고 있고, 비록 현재
   중단된 상태이나 남북한간 5-6개의 대화 채널이 실재하고 있음에
   비추어 유엔사무총장의 남북한간 중재역할의 여지가 그렇게 클
   것으로 보이지 않음.

o 또한 금후 결의안 채택을 추진할 경우 동 내용에 따라 달라지겠
   으나, 어떠한 경우에라도 북한측이 대응해 올 가능성을 지나치게
   과소평가한 감이 있음.

0049

면 담 요 록

1. 일시 및 장소
   - 1차 : 1990.4.16(월) 10:40-11:20, 차관실
   - 2차 : 1990.4.16(월) 19:00-19:30, 만찬장

2. 면 담 자 : 유종하 외무차관
   Eric Suy 벨기에 외상 고문

3. 배   석 : 이시영 대사, 송영식 국제기구조약국장,
   이규형 국제연합과장, (1차 면담시 김대식 통상 2과장,
   신각수 차관 보좌관 동석)

4. 면담내용 : (한국의 유엔가입 문제 중심)

   (1차 면담초 차관의 벨기에 외상에 대한 안부 문의 및 이에 대한
   수이교수의 전언이 있었고, 양국 기후 및 수이 교수의 체한일정에
   관하여 환담이 있었음.)

   차 관 : 이제 본론에 들어가 유엔가입 문제에 관하여 의견을
           교환코자 함. 송국장 면담시 조금 이야기가 있었는지.

   고 문 : 잠시 있었음. 북한측이 금년만해도 안보리 문서를 3회
           돌렸다고 들었는데, 2개 Korea 의 유엔가입 불용인 입장에
           변화는 없겠지요.

0050

차 관 : 그들 입장에 관하여 소측이 주로 알려온 사항이지만 몇몇
루머는 있음. 현재 그들은 한.미간 팀스피릿트 훈련을
이유로 남북대화를 중단시키고 있는 바, 훈련이 종료되게
되면 불원 대화에 응해오리라 보는데, 루머에 의하면
북한측은 유엔문제에 관하여 특별한 제안을 하리라는 것임.
동 내용은 고체대표권(Alternative Membership)과 같은
것이라 함. 아마도 북한과 소련과의 협의를 거친것 같은데,
동 문제에 관한 북한측 입장이 불변화라는 전제에서 출발한
것으로 생각됨.

고 문 : 소련은 북한의 변화를 원하고 있을 것임. 미측 입장은.

차 관 : 미측은 최근 한국문제를 총회에 제기하는 문제를 검토해
볼수 있다는 생각임.

고 문 : 비공식적인 북한대표단이 언젠가 카네기재단 후원으로
미국을 방문한 것으로 아는데.

이대사 : 작년도에 학술회의 참석차 미국을 방문한 적이 있음.

0051

고 문 : 무슨 논의가 없었는지.

차 관 : 없었음. 금년에는 스텐포드 대학측과의 학술회의에
외고부 부부장급이 참석할 예정이었으나 취소되었음.
동 모임에는 우리도 초청받아 관계 학자가 참석 예정
이었으나, 북한측은 마지막 단계에서 마음을 바꾸었음.

대 사 : 동 회의가 열렸다면 남북한 및 미국이 참석하는 3자
회의가 되었을 것임.

차 관 : 그와 유사한 것으로 요미우리 신문이 주최하는 세미나
에도 남북한이 초청되고 있음.

고 문 : 여러가지 질문을 드린 것은 한국의 유엔가입 문제에 관한
최근의 변화가 없었는가 하는 이유에서 였음.
유엔회원국이 되고자 할 경우 안보리의 권고가 불가피한
바, 안보리에는 중국과 소련이 있다는 점을 간과할 수
없음. 물론 가입권고 채택에 필요한 9개국 찬성은 가능할
것으로 보나, 동시에 1개 또는 2개의 거부권이 행사될
가능성이 상존함.
    그간 중국의 변화 가능성에 관한 아무런 시사가
없으며, 만약 중국측이 (한국가입 문제와 관련) 거부권을
행사한다면 이는 분명 정치적 이유에서 사용하는 것인 바,
동 결과 한.중 관계가 후퇴하게 될 것임.

0052

한편, 유엔가입 문제와 관련 한국문제에 관한 총회
의제하에서 (회원국들로 하여금) 논의를 하게 하는 방법도
있음. 즉 유엔의 보편성 원칙에 반하는 현재의 비정상적인
상황을 종식시키기 위하여 한국측이 회원국들에 대한
외교적 노력을 적극 전개할 경우, 총회에서 Debate 는
여러가지 측면에서 좋은 결과를 가져올 수 있을 것임.
가입문제는 1차적으로 안보리 소관이라는 점을 감안할때
Debate의 결과 추진될 결의안은 가입문제에 국한할 것이
아니라 남북한 관계도 함께 다루는 것이 좋을 것임.

　　즉 용어 선택을 잘하여 추진해야 할 결의안 내용으로는
가령 유엔사무총장으로 하여금 한반도 문제에 관하여 중재
(Good office)를 하도록 요청하는 것이 고려될 수 있을
것임. 실제 유엔사무총장은 남북대화를 도와줄 의향이
있을 것이므로 이를 보다 적극적으로 활용할 경우
아프가니스탄 사태 해결에서의 예와 같이 몇년후 좋은
결과를 기대할 수도 있음. 이와 같이 사무총장을 한국문제
해결을 위하여 적극 활용하자는 까닭은 모든 유엔회원국이
사무총장 이외에는 어떠한 누구도 문제를 해결하지 못한
다는 점을 인식케 하고, 그에 따라 유엔사무총장이 점진적
으로 문제해결을 도모하여 궁극적으로는 지금당장 추진할
경우 거부권이 행사될 것이 분명한 남북한 유엔가입문제를
최종단계에서 해결하자는데 있음.

0053

차 관 : 동건관련 설명드릴 것이 있음.

　　　　우리는 최근 7개 동구권 국가와 수교하였으며, 알제리 및
　　　　나미비아와도 외교관계를 맺었음. 이에 따라 유엔회원국중
　　　　전통적으로 북한을 지지해온 35-6개 국가중 적어도 10여개
　　　　국가가 과거의 확실한 북한지지 입장을 변경할 것으로
　　　　보며, 반면 우리의 경우 종전 80여개의 지지국수에 10여개
　　　　국이 증가될 것으로 예상함. 또한 안보리 상임이사국중
　　　　소련은 그간 태도를 변경하여 기권할 것으로 기대되고
　　　　있음. 적어도 소련은 유엔문제에 관한한 한.소 관계
　　　　현황보다 앞선 입장을 보여주고 있다고 판단함.
　　　　물론 진짜 투표가 있을 경우 어떨지 확신할 수 없으나,
　　　　아마 기권할 것이라는 생각임.

고 문 : 보편성 원칙을 강조하는등 최근 소측의 태도에 긍정적인
　　　　측면이 있으므로 차관님 견해가 타당하다고 생각함.

차 관 : 소측과는 직접.간접적으로 대화를 할 수 있고, 또한
　　　　미측을 통하여 태도를 확인할 수 있음. 앞으로 경제분야
　　　　에서의 협력증진등 점진적인 관계개선의 단계를 거치면서
　　　　유엔문제 해결은 더욱 쉬어지리라는 인식임. 따라서 금후
　　　　총회에 문제를 제기하여 아측입장을 지지하는 압도적인
　　　　표세를 과시하고, 동시에 북한측 지지 세력이 감소되고
　　　　있다는 사실을 보여줄 수 있는 방안을 검토코자 함.

공　　　란

고 문 : 금후 결정한다면 투표대상이 될 결의안은 무엇을 답을
       것인지. (한국문제에 관한) 일반적인 사항이 될 것인지?

차 관 : 절차적 측면에서도 적합한 내용이어야 할 것임. 다만
       다만 전반적인 한국문제에 관한 것보다는 가입문제에
       국한된 내용을 생각하고 있음. 우리는 이미 북한측과
       한국문제 불상정 원칙을 합의한 바 있으며, 한국문제를
       유엔에 가져가는 것은 문제해결에 별 도움이 되지 않을
       것으로 생각함. 또한 우리는 유엔에서 남북 대결을
       원하지 않음.

고 문 : 유엔가입 문제로 국한할 경우 범위가 좁지 않을지.

차 관 : 총회에 제출한 결의안 내용으로는 상금 미결중인 한국의
       유엔가입 문제를 안보리가 재검토해 줄 것을 요청하는
       것을 생각할 수 있을 것임.

고 문 : 솔직히 말씀드리면 동 결의안을 둘러싸고 Debate가 벌어
       질텐데, 차관이 북한을 확고하게 지지하는 국가가 25-30
       개국 밖에 되지 않는다고 하였지만, 아마도 그들 국가들은
       틀림없이 가입문제는 안보리의 소관사항인데 왜 총회에
       제기하는가라는 식으로 우선 기술적, 절차적, 법적 측면
       에서의 문제점을 제기해 올 것임.

0056

차 관 : 물론 그렇게 추진하고자 할 경우 사전에 조치할 사항이
많을 것이며, 또한 쉬운문제가 아니라는 점도 알고 있음.
이와 관련 우리의 가입문제를 안보리에 제기하는 방안도
배제하지 않는다는 점을 말씀드리고자 함. 중요한 것은
우리가 북한측이 반대한다고 하여 가입실현 노력을 하지
않는 것은 북한측에게 거부권을 주는 것과 다름없다는
점임.

이대사 : 실제 상황에 들어가면 결의안을 제출하되 투표는 하지않는
방안도 검토할 수 있을 것임.

고 문 : 한국문제를 Debate 하려면 총회가 적합한 것인 바, 25-30
개국의 확고한 북측 지지국도 고려해야 할 것임.

이대사 : 가입 안건을 총회에 막바로 제기하는데 따른 기술적인
문제점도 신중히 검토해야 한다고 봄.

차 관 : 다음 예정된 일정상 이만 마쳐야 되겠음. 저녁 만찬시
조금 일찍 만나 더 논의하는 것이 좋겠음.

0057

(2차 면담시 언급내용)

차 관 : 오전에 나누었던 이야기를 계속하기로 함. 유엔가입
문제와 관련 한가지 공통적인 인식은 한.소관계 수립이
금년 또는 늦어도 내년중에 이루어질 것이며, 만약 중국이
(우리의 유엔가입 문제에 대하여) 거부권을 행사한다면
그것은 유일한 거부권이 되리라는 점임. 또한 중국은
소련이 거부권을 행사하지 않을 경우, 그와 같이 좋지
않은 짓을 재차 하는 것을 꺼려하게 될 것임.

고 문 : 안보리의 여타 이사국 태도는 어떻게 보고 있는지.

차 관 : 최소한 9개국 이상의 찬성은 있을 것임.

고 문 : 그 이상도 가능할 것임. 그런데 지금 말씀하신 것은
안보리에서의 시나리오인지.

차 관 : 안보리도 충분히 생각해야 함. 총회에 가기전에 안보리를
통과해야 한다는 점도 있으므로 거부권이 행사될 위험이
따르더라도 안보리에 제기하는 것도 고려해야 함.
그뒤 총회에 재심을 청구하는 형식이 되지 않을까 생각함.

고 문 : 개인적인 견해이나 그와 같은 것은 매우 위험한 게임이라고
생각함. 물론 총회가 안보리의 권고를 받아서 회원국의
가입 결정을 하는 것이지만, 안보리에서 권고가 되지 않은
것을 총회에 제기한다는 것은 매우 위험한 것으로 봄.

0058

차 관 : 과거에도 있었음. 2차례에 걸쳐

이대사 : 안보리토의 이후에 총회에 제기한 적도 있었고, 안보리
토의없이 막바로 총회에 제기한 경우도 있었음.

고 문 : 회원국 가입건이 아닌한 문제가 없을 것임. 그러나
막바로 총회에 제기하는 것은 Risky 함. 제 생각은 가입
문제가 아닌 것으로 회원국들의 태도를 테스트 해보는
것이 좋다고 생각함. 물론 한국문제 불상정 원칙에 대한
합의가 있다고 하지만, 총회 의제를 잘 만들어 낸다면
문제없을 것임.

이대사 : 우리는 한국문제의 재론을 피하는 입장임.
가입 문제가 아닌 전반적인 한국문제에 관한 안건이 있게
되면 남.북한이 각자 우방국을 동원할 것이므로 비생산적
이고 대결적인 논쟁의 재연은 불가피할 것임.

고 문 : 결의안 내용에 달려 있음. 즉 한국문제 전반을 토의하자는
것이 아님을 분명히 하고, 단지 사무총장의 중재(Good
office)를 요청하는 내용으로 할 경우 아무도 과거 문제의
재탕이라고 보지 않을 것임.

이대사 : 북한측은 단순히 밸런스를 위하여서라도 분명 그러한
결의안에 대응하는 결의안 제출을 시도할 것임.

0059

고　문 : 그렇게 간단치는 않을 것임.

　　　　만약 동 결의안이 남북한간 대화를 위한 사무총장의 중재를
　　　　요청하는 내용에 촛점을 맞춘다면 북한측의 대항 결의안
　　　　제출은 어려울 것임.

송국장 : 가입문제를 언급치 않는 결의안은 별의미 없을 것임.

고　문 : 결의안 제출 목적을 잘 설명하면, 즉 "가입 달성을 위하여
　　　　등등"하면 될 것임.

송국장 : 그렇지만 직접 언급치 않을 경우 큰 의미를 가질 수 있을
　　　　런지 의문임.

이대사 : 이제 팀스피리트훈련이 끝나면 남북대화가 재개될 것으로
　　　　보임. 따라서 수이교수가 말한 내용으로 결의안을 추진
　　　　한다면 일부에서는 남북대화가 이루어지고 있는데 뭣때문에
　　　　사무총장이 나서야 하는지에 의문을 제기할 것임.

고　문 : 사무총장의 역할을 생각하면 해답이 나올수 있을 것임.
　　　　사무총장은 그간 국제적 주요 난제를 성공적으로 해결함에
　　　　따라 그 능력에 대한 신뢰감이 고양되었고, 카리스마적인
　　　　영향력을 가지게 되었음.

　　　　　또한 사무총장은 이제 한국문제가 다음번 해결되어야
　　　　할 문제로 생각하고 있으며, 특히 동 문제해결에 적극적인
　　　　의사를 가지고 있다고 봄.

0060

그간 남북한간 체육 및 문화부문에서 직접 접촉이
있었으나 사무총장의 중재가 있을 경우 동 결과는 달라질
것임.

이대사 : 총리 회담을 위한 예비 실무자회담도 있고 국회회담도
있음.

차 관 : 그런데 안보리에서 비토될 경우 왜 총회에 제기하는 것이
위험(Risky)하다고 보는지.

고 문 : 확실히 기억나지 않지만, 안보리의 역할은 그간 변하여
왔음. 그간의 결의안들을 보면 안보리가 유엔내에서
보다 중심적인 역할을 해야 한다는 분위기가 일반적이며,
회원국도 이를 잘 알고 있음. 따라서 안보리가 해야 할
일을 총회가 대신한다는 것은 안보리에 대한 도전이라고
보여질 것임.

이대사 : 안보리 토의후 총회 결의안 채택추진시 대략 두가지 주요
내용을 생각할 수 있음. 즉 한국가입 당위성을 지적하고,
안보리가 이를 재검토해 줄 것을 요청하는 내용을 생각할
수 있을 것임.

고 문 : 재검토 해줄 것을 요청하기 위하여는 보다 현실적이어야
함. 한국이 유엔가입 요건을 충족하고 있다는 등등은
굳이 언급할 필요는 없을 것임.

0061

이대사 : 전문 파트에라도 넣는 것이 좋지 않을지.

고 문 : 꼭 넣고 싶은지.

이대사 : 자격 문제에 대한 언급은 필요하리라 보는데.

고 문 : 보편성 원칙만 언급하면 충분하다고 봄. 굳이 자격을
강조할 필요는 없을 것임.

이대사 : 물론 북한 체면을 살려주는 타협적인 결의안이여야 한다고
생각함.

고 문 : 거부권을 행사하기 어려운 내용으로 해야 함.

차 관 : 시간 관계상 협의를 중단해야 할것 같음. 토요일까지
계시니까 금후 일정을 감안 이시영 대사와 좀더 협의해
주길 바람. 끝.

0062

아국 유엔가입 관련 추진방안 검토

제 1안 : 아국가입 촉구 총회결의안 추진

추진계획	○ 총회에서 아국 유엔가입 촉구 내용의 결의안을 "신규회원 가입" 의제하에 우방국들이 제출, 채택토록 함.
장　　점	○ 아국 유엔가입에 대한 국제적 지지기반 확인 ○ 소.중의 거부권 부재 및 기권, 불참등 투표태도 변화 기대 가능 ○ 대다수 찬성으로 채택시 소.중 및 북한에 대한 압력 작용 가능
단　　점	○ 유엔에서의 남북한 대결 재연 (아국의 화해지향 정책과 모순) 　－ 압도적 찬성표 확보 부담(단순한 결의채택만으로는 의미부족) 　－ 북한의 대응 의제 또는 결의안을 부결시켜야 하는 부담 ○ 북방외교에 대한 부정적 영향 가능 ○ 가입문제가 안보리의 1차적 관할사항임에 비추어, 아국가입 문제도 안보리의 재심의가 선행되어야 한다는 절차적 논란 가능
제출 결의안 내용	○ 전문 : － 최근의 화해.협력 지향 국제 조류로 유엔의 역할 증대 필요성이 높아지고, 유엔회원권의 보편성 원칙이 강조되고 있음. 　　　　－ 대한민국은 유엔회원국 자격을 충족하고 있으며, 이는 유엔총회 결의등으로 확인된 바 있음. 　　　　－ 대한민국의 가입문제는 과거 안보리에서 정치적 이유로 인한 상임이사국간의 의견 불일치로 타결되지 못하였는 바, 이제는 그러한 국제적 사정이 변화 되었음. 　　　　－ 대한민국의 유엔가입은 대한민국의 국제사회에 대한 기여를 증진함과 동시에 남북한 통일까지의 과도적 조치로서 한반도 평화와 통일의 촉진에 이바지할 것임을 확신함. 　　　　－ 대한민국과 함께 북한의 유엔가입도 환영할 것임. ○ 본문 : － 안보리가 상기를 감안, 대한민국의 가입문제를 재고 합하여 줄 것을 촉구함. 　　　　－ 남북한과 관련 당사국들이 한반도의 긴장완화와 평화 정착 및 궁극적인 평화통일을 위한 협상을 적극 추진 할 것을 촉구함.

0063

북한측 예상반응	o 대응결의안 제출 가능
	
	  - "신규회원 가입" 의제하에서 남북한 통일후 가입촉구등
	    내용의 결의안 또는 수정안 제출
	
	  - 한반도 문제의 부활 (예 : 1975년 한국문제 관련 결의의
	    이행)을 유발하는 의제 및 외군철수 결의안 제출
	
	  * 북한의 부담 : 자신의 수정안에 대한 2/3 찬성 확보 또는
	              외군 철수 결의안에 대한 75년 수준 찬성
	              확보 부담
	
	o 아측결의안 부결 책동 예상 (기권표 동원 공작 포함)

0064

제 2안 : 안보리 제기후 총회결의안 추진

추진계획	ㅇ 안보리에 아국가입 문제를 재상정, 표결에 의한 부결(소.중 거부권행사) 또는 토의후 표결 보류의 과정을 거침. ㅇ 상기 안보리 심의결과 (총회에 보고서 제출)를 토대로, 우방국 들이 아측가입을 위한 안보리의 재심 요청 내용의 총회 결의안을 제출, 채택토록 함.
장 점	ㅇ (제 1안의 장점에 추가로) 총회 결의안 우선 추진시 야기될 수 있는 절차적 논란 봉쇄 ㅇ 안보리에서 소.중이 거부권 불행사시 아국가입 실현 가능
단 점	ㅇ 아국가입 문제의 안보리 재상정은 거부권 행사를 위요, 소.중을 딜렘마에 봉착케 할 것이므로, 아국으로서는 제 1안 보다 신중한 외교적 고려가 필요함. ㅇ 안보리에서의 아국가입 부결은 외교정책의 실패로 비추어질 수 있는 정치적 부담이 있음.
제출결의안 내용	ㅇ 제 1안 내용과 동일하되, 전문에 "안보리의 한국가입 문제 심의 결과 보고서에 유의함." 표현 추가
북한측 예상반응	ㅇ 제 1안과 같은 반응 예상

0065

제 3안 : 보편성원칙 강조 총회결의안 추진 (Suy 교수 제시방안)

추진계획	ㅇ 유엔총회 "신규회원가입" 의제하에서 아국을 특별히 거명하지 않고 유엔회원권의 보편성원칙을 강조하는 내용의 결의안을 제출, 채택토록 함.
장 점	ㅇ 아국은 거명치 않고 일반적으로 보편성 원칙을 강조함으로써 북한 및 동조국들의 반대책동이 어려워짐. ㅇ 가입희망 의사에 반하여 유엔에 가입치 못하고 있는 국가가 아국 뿐이므로, 결과적으로 아국가입 당위성 확산에 기여
단 점	ㅇ 아국을 거명치 않은 보편성원칙의 일반적 거론은 아국가입 문제에 대한 여론 환기 효과가 감소됨. (북한측도 이론적으로는 보편성 원칙을 반대하는 것이 아니라 보편성 원칙의 분단국 비적용을 주장하고 있음을 감안 필요) ㅇ 보편성원칙의 일반적 거론내용은 그러한 원칙적이고 당연한 내용의 결의안이 성립할 수 있느냐에 대한 의문부터 야기가능 ㅇ 결의안 채택을 위한 외교적 노력은 여전히 필요하며, 북한이 동 결의안에 반대치 않는 경우 아측 부담은 줄지만 결의안 채택 의미 별무
제출 결의안	ㅇ 전문 : - 최근 국제사회의 평화.협력 지향 분위기로 유엔의 역할 강화 필요성이 강조됨. 　　　　 - 유엔의 목적.이상을 효과적으로 달성키 위해서는 모든 국가의 유엔 참여가 필요함. ㅇ 본문 : - 유엔헌장에 구현된 회원권의 보편성원칙을 재확인 하며, 유엔가입을 희망하고 자격을 갖춘 모든국가의 가입 실현을 촉구함.
북한측 예상반응	ㅇ 총회결의안 내용이 아국가입 문제를 암시한다는 이유로 채택 부결 책동 가능 　　　 - 상기가 불가능시, 결의안 내용을 희석시켜 아국과의 연관성을 극소화 시키려고 시도 가능 ㅇ 북한도 보편성원칙 자체는 지지하므로 아측 결의안을 반대하지 않는다고 하고, 다만 이러한 내용이 분단국에는 적용되지 않는 다고 유보를 표명하는 식의 전술 구사 가능

0066

제 4안 : 유엔사무총장의 중재 요청 총회결의안 추진 (Suy 교수 제시 방안)

추진계획	ㅇ 한반도문제, 특히 남북한 유엔가입 문제와 관련하여, "신규회원 가입" 또는 별도 의제하에 사무총장의 중재 (good office)를 요청하는 내용의 총회결의안을 제출, 채택토록 함.
장 점	ㅇ 아국입장에 대한 지지가 아닌 유엔사무총장의 중재요청 내용에 대하여 북한 및 동조국들이 반대하기가 어려워짐. ㅇ 아국가입 문제에 대한 여론 환기 효과는 어느 정도 있음. ㅇ 유엔사무총장이 남북한의 유엔가입을 긍정적으로 보는 경우, 아국입장이 더욱 강화됨.
단 점	ㅇ 유엔사무총장이 가입문제는 안보리의 1차적 관할사항이라는 점에서 동 결의안 추진에 부정적 태도를 보일 가능성이 있음. (44차 총회 아국 외무장관 면담시 사무총장은 아국 가입에는 안보리 상임이사국들의 태도가 중요하다고 언급) ㅇ 설사 사무총장이 중재에 나서더라도 사무총장으로서는 아국에만 유리한 방향의 입장을 취할 수는 없을 것임. ㅇ 남북한이 한반도문제의 당사자 해결 원칙을 주장하고 있음과 모순되며, 남북대화가 재개되면 사무총장의 개입여지가 없어질 수 있음.
제출결의안 내용	ㅇ 전문 : - 최근 국제정세와 유엔의 역할 강화 필요성 및 보편성 원칙에 비추어, 한반도문제, 특히 남북한의 유엔 대표권 문제의 해결이 모색되어야 할 시점에 왔음. ㅇ 본문 : - 이와 관련, 유엔사무총장이 남북한과 협의하여 중재 역할을 수행하여 주고, 차기 총회에 보고서를 제출하여 줄 것을 요청함.
북한측 예상반응	ㅇ 유엔내에서 가입문제의 관할권, 한반도문제의 당사자 해결 원칙을 들어, 반대책동 가능

0067

아국가입 촉구 유엔총회 결의안에 대한 예상표세 분석

90. 4. 20. 국제연합과

구 분	지 지 예 상	불 확 실	반 대 예 상
안보리이사국 (15)	미국, 영국, 불란서, 카나다, 말련, 자이르, 콜롬비아, 코트디브와르, 핀랜드 (9)	소련, 남예맨, 루마니아 (3)	중국, 쿠바, 이디오피아 (3)
아 주 (23)	일본, 태국, 파키스탄, 필리핀, PNG, 휘지, 솔로몬아일랜드, 방글라데시, 스리랑카, 싱가폴, 서사모아, 부탄, 브루나이, 네팔, 몰디브 (15)	인도, 인니, 미얀마, 바누아투, 몽고 (5)	라오스, 베트남, 캄푸챠 (3)
서구 및 기타 (19)	터키, 서독, 덴마크, 벨기에, 뉴질랜드, 호주, 희랍, 화란, 아일랜드, 몰타*, 놀웨이, 오지리, 룩셈부르크, 폴투갈, 아이슬랜드, 스페인, 이태리 (17)	스웨덴, 사이프러스 (2)	
중 남 미 (31)	알젠틴, 도미니카(공), 볼리비아, 우루과이, 바하마, 과데말라, 트리니다드토바고, 칠레, 그레나다, 수리남, 세인트빈센트, 아이티, 도미니카(연), 멕시코, 엘살바돌, 온두라스, 세인트키츠네비스, 안티구아 바부다, 에쿠아돌, 코스타리카, 파라과이, 바베이도스, 파나마 (23)	페루, 자마이카, 브라질, 베네수엘라, 벨리즈, 가이아나, 세인트루시아 (7)	니카라과 (1)

0068

구 분	지 지 예 상	불 확 실	반 대 예 상
중 동 (21)	바레인, 카탈, 튀니지, 요르단, 쿠웨이트, 수단, 사우디, 이라크, 모로코, UAE, 오만, 북예멘 (12)	모리타니아, 레바논, 이스라엘, 리비아, 이란, 이집트 (6)	시리아, 알제리, 아프가니스탄 (3)
아프리카 (42)	감비아, 나이제리아, 니제, 카메룬, 가봉, 소말리아, 케냐, 적도기니, 라이베리아, 모리셔스, 시에라레온, 스와질랜드, 중앙아, 상토메프린시페 (14)	세네갈, 가나, 레소토, 루안다, 보츠와나, 코모로, 캅베르데, 남아공, 모잠비크, 챠드, 우간다, 지부티, 말라위, 기네비소, 나미비아 (15)	기네, 부르키나파소, 세이셸, 앙골라, 잠비아, 짐바브웨, 콩고, 토고, 부룬디, 탄자니아, 말리, 베냉, 마다가스칼 (13)
동 구 (9)	헝가리 (1)	불가리아, 체코, 유고, 폴란드, 백러시아, 우크라이나 (6)	알바니아, 동독 (2)
계	91	44	25

* 분석기준

　1988년 제 43차 유엔총회시 아국대표 총회연설 의제의 표결에 대비한

　고섭결과 예상 표세 분석을 토대로, 그간 아국과의 관계개선 국가의

　투표성향 변화 가능성등을 반영하여 보완함.

0069

안보리 결의안(I)

91. 4. 18.
국제연합과

(304)

1. 결의안에 포함되어야 할 사항

　ㅇ 아국의 가입을 총회에 권고
　　- 안보리 결의안은 구체적 조치를 포함하여야 하므로 한국의 가입을
　　　총회에 권고하는 내용을 골자로 함.
　　　(한국이 가입요건을 충족시키고 있다는 선언적 내용을 담은 결의안은
　　　총회 결의안으로는 적합할지 모르나 안보리 결의안으로는 부적절함)

　ㅇ 안보리가 동 결의안을 채택한 근거 제시
　　- 안보리가 아국의 가입을 권고하는 근거로서 1949년 이래 아국의
　　　유엔가입문제가 안보리에 계류되어 있음을 감안, 동 신청을 재검토한
　　　조치임을 명기

　ㅇ 아국의 가입문제가 해결되어야 하는 시대적 요청(배경) 설명
　　- 화해와 화합의 신국제질서하에서 냉전의 유산을 제거하기 위한 조치

　ㅇ 유엔의 보편성원칙 강조

　ㅇ 북한의 가입 권고
　　- 북한 및 중국의 입장에 대한 배려

　ㅇ 남북대화 노력 촉구
　　- 유엔가입문제와 남북대화의 연계는 배제

　ㅇ 한반도의 긴장완화, 평화정착과 남북한 통일을 위한 관련국들의 협조 촉구
　　- 국제평화와 안전유지에 1차적 책임을 지는 안보리의 결의안으로서의
　　　balance 유지상 필요

2. 결의안 제안국 : 아국의 우방국 (미.영.불등)

0070

3. 유의사항

ㅇ 결의안의 성격

　　- 아국의 가입권고 결의안임을 명백히 함.

ㅇ 중국의 입장 고려

　　- 아국의 가입을 권고함과 동시에 북한의 가입을 촉구함으로써 아측
　　　만의 단독가입을 노리고 있다는 우려 불식

ㅇ Double Veto 문제

　　- 결의안 작성시 단순히 선언적 또는 원칙론적 내용만을 밝힐 경우
　　　중국의 찬성 또는 기권을 비교적 용이하게 확보할 수도 있으나 반대로
　　　중국이 동 원칙론적 결의안에도 Veto를 할 수 있고, 추후 아측의
　　　가입신청서 제출에 따른 심의시에도 Veto를 할 수 있어 아국가입
　　　문제에 대해 double veto권을 주는 결과가 됨. (즉, 선언적 성격의
　　　결의안에 대한 중국의 찬성 또는 기권이 구체적 가입신청시 동일
　　　하게 찬성 또는 기권으로 연결되리라는 보장이 없으므로 가입실현을
　　　위해 불필요한 절차를 추가하는 결과가 될 우려)

　　- 특히 선언적 성격의 결의안이 중국의 건설적 역할을 보다 용이하게
　　　촉구할 수 있는 방안도 되겠으나 다른 한편으로는

　　　ⅰ) 동안에 대한 찬성 또는 기권의 댓가로서 금년중 우리로부터
　　　　　가입신청을 않겠다는 보장을 요구하거나

　　　ⅱ) 또는 우리의 가입신청에 대한 veto 사용보다 동 결의안에 대한
　　　　　veto 사용이 국제사회에서 중국의 입장을 덜 손상한다는 판단
　　　　　(판단근거 : non-interference 원칙에 따라 강대국이 남북한의
　　　　　가입문제에 대해 간섭 불가)하에 veto를 사용키로 결정할 가능성도
　　　　　있음.

0071

Draft Resolution (I)

(권고)

The Security Council,

Noting with satisfaction the recent trend under the improved international atmosphere to strengthen the role of the United Nations in resolving regional conflicts and promoting international peace and security,

Bearing in mind that the role of the United Nations can best be enhanced when all States qualified for membership according to Article 4 of the Charter and willing to join are admitted to the Organization in conformity with the principle of universality,

Having reexamined the pending application of the Republic of Korea for admission to the United Nation,

Noting with regret that the Republic of Korea has been denied its membership in the United Nations for the last four decades against its strong wish and despite its qualification,

Considering that the admission of the Republic of Korea to the United Nations would not only reduce tension in and around the Korean peninsula and facilitate the process of inter-Korean reconciliation toward the goal of reunification, but also enable the Republic of Korea to contribute to the work of the Organizations,

Further considering that the admission of the Republic of Korea,
as an interim measure pending reunification of Korea, does not prejudice
either the subsequent admission of the Democratic People's Republic of
Korea if and whenever it so desires, or an eventual single membership
in the United Nations when the Republic of Korea and the Democratic
Peoples Republic of Korea are reunified,

1. Recommends to the General Assembly that the Republic of Korea be admitted to membership in the United Nations;

2. Calls upon the two Korean Governments to accelerate their dialogues and negotiations for reconciliation and reunification;

3. Invites the Democratic People's Republic of Korea to join membership in the United Nations at an earlies possible date;

4. Also invites the Governments concerned to cooperate closely among themselves and with the two Korean Governments in order to create in and around the Korean peninsula conditions conducive to the normalization of relations, peace and stability in the region, and peaceful reunification of Korea.

0073

Draft Resolution(Ⅱ)

(초안)

The Security Council,

Noting with satisfaction the recent improved international atmosphere and the trend to strengthen the role of the United Nations in resolving regional conflicts and promoting international peace and cooperation.

Bearing in mind that the role of the United Nations can best be enhanced when all States participate in the work of the Organization in conformity with the principle of universality,

Recalling the applications of the Democratic People's Republic of Korea and the Republic of Korea for membership in the United Nations still remain unresolved,

Convinced that the principle of universality implies that all States qualified for membership according to Article 4 of the Charter and willing to join should be admitted to the Organization,

Considering in particular the United Nations membership of divided nations does not prejudice either their efforts for reunification or an eventual single membership after their reunification,

1. Invites the Democratic People's Republic of Korea and the Republic of Korea to renew their application for admission to the United Nations to participate as Member States in the work of the Organization;

2. Further invites the two Korean Governments to accelerate their dialogue and negoiations for reconciliation and reunification;

0074

3. Calls upon the Governments concerned to cooperate closely among themselves and with the two Korean Governments in order to create in and around the Korean peninsula conditions conducive to the normalization of relations, peace and stability in the region, and peaceful reunification of Korea.

0075

Draft Resolution

The Security Council,

Noting with satisfaction the recent trend under the improved
international atmosphere to strengthen the role of the United Nations
in resolving regional conflicts and promoting international peace and
security,

Bearing in mind that the role of the United Nations can best be
enhanced when any State qualified for membership according to Article 4
of the Charter and willing to join is admitted to the Organization in
conformity with the principle of universality,

Noting with regret that the Republic of Korea has been denied its
membership in the United Nations for the last four decades against its
strong wish and despite its qualification,

Considering that virtual consensus has emerged within the international
community that the Republic of Korea should join the United Nations to assume
its due responsibilities in further promoting international peace and security
and enhancing well-being of mankind,

Further considering that the admission of the Republic of Korea,
as an interim measure pending reunification of Korea, does not prejudice
either the subsequent admission of the Democratic People's Republic of
Korea if and whenever it so desires, or an eventual single membership

0076

in the United Nations when the Republic of Korea and the Democratic
People's Republic of Korea are reunified, rather facilitate the process
of reunification of both Koreas,

1. Recommends to the General Assembly that the Republic of Korea be
   admitted to membership in the United Nations;

2. Invites the Democratic People's Republic of Korea to join membership
   in the United Nations at an earliest possible date ;

3. Calls upon the Democratic People's Republic of Korea and the Republic
   of Korea to strengthen their efforts to promote peace and security in
   the Korean peninsula and accelerate the process of reunification on
   the basis of reconciliation and rapprochement with a view to attaining
   an eventual single membership after their reunification.

0077

정 리 보 존 문 서 목 록					
기록물종류	일반공문서철	등록번호	2020060120	등록일자	2020-06-29
분류번호	731.12	국가코드		보존기간	영구
명 칭	남북한 유엔가입, 1991.9.17. 전41권				
생 산 과	국제연합1과	생산년도	1990~1991	담당그룹	
권 차 명	V.7 한국의 기본입장 각서(Memorandum) 안보리문서 배포				
내용목차	* 유엔가입 추진관련 정부 기본입장을 안보리 문서로 배포 　- 4.5일 안보리의장에게 각서 전달, 4.8 안보리 문서(S/22455)로 배포				

0001

관리 번호	91 -644

발 신 전 보

번 호 : <u>WUN-0462</u>   910308 1621 FD 종별: 지급

수 신 : 주 유연   대사. /총영사 대리

발 신 : 장 관 (국연)

제 목 : 유연가입 추진(메모랜덤)

연 : WUN-0459

연호관련, 금후 적절한 계기에 유연가입에 관한 아국입장을 안보리문서로
배포함과동시에 이를 각국에 대한 고섭시 사용코자 하는 것이 좋을 것으로
사료되는 바, 동 Memorandum(안)을 작성, 가능한 3.11(월)중 본부 타전바람.

끝.

검토필(1991. 6. 30)

예고 : ..에 예고
예고 인반 1991.12.31. 일반.

(국제기구조약국장   문동석)

앙 고 재	91 년 3 월 8 일	4 N 과	기안자 성명	과 장	국 장	차 관	장 관
					전결		

보 안 통 제	

외신과통제

0002

분류번호 보존기간

발 신 전 보

번   호 : WUN-0463   910308 1623 FD 종별 : 지급

수   신 : 주 유엔   대사. /총영사/ (서대원 참사관)

발   신 : 장   관 (국연과 이규형 배)

제   목 : 업   연

연 : WUN-0462

(국제기구조약국장
친전22)

연호, 주말에 연락을 드려 죄송하오나 가급적 3.11(월) 오전중에 본부에

송착토록 하여 주시기바람.   끝.

1.8 예 고 : 독후파기

		기안자 성명		과 장		국 장		차 관	장 관
앙 고 재	91년 3월 8일	4개과	서영화						

보 안 통 제

외신과통제

공　　　란

공   란

공   란

남북한 유엔 가입 총회결안 추진 및 기본입장 각서

공 란

공   란

남북한 유엔 가입 총회결안 추진 및 기본입장 각서

공   란

공   란

남북한 유엔 가입 총회결안 추진 및 기본입장 각서

공　　　란

공   란

공　　　　　　란

분류번호	보존기간

발 신 전 보

WUN-0618   910322 1922 FG   종별: 지급

번 호 :

수 신 : 주   유엔   대사.♣♣♣♣♣

발 신 : 장 관   (국연)

제 목 : 아국입장 안보리문서 배포

대 : UNW-580(1), UNW-0634(2)

1. 대호(1)관련, 유엔가입문제에 관한 각서를 안보리문서로 배포하는 시기는 본부도 3월말경이 적절하다고 보고 있음.

2. 다만 각서 내용과 관련, 현재 본부에서 다각도로 검토, 작성중에 있어 대호 면담시 아측안을 제시하기가 어려운 사정임.

3. 따라서 대호(2) Pickering 미대사 예방면담시 상기 1항 계획에 관해 의견교환을 갖는 설명하는 한편, 각서안에 대해서는 현재 본부에서 내용 검토중이며 작성 완료되는대로 미측과 협의 예정임을 적의 언급바람.

끝.

(국제기구조약국장 문동석)

검토필(1991. 6. 30)

보 안 통 제	예

앙 고 재	91 년 3 월 22 일	유엔과	기안자 성명		과 장		국 장		차 관	장 관	외신과통제
					예		전결				

관리 번호	91 -1006

외 무 부

종 별 :

번 호 : UNW-0713   일 시 : 91 0327 1900

수 신 : 장관(유엔과장)

발 신 : 주 유엔 서 대원

제 목 : 업연

  1. 각서건 진전사항 참고로 회시바람.

  2. 혹시 궁금할까 하여, UNW-0702 2 항 다의 QUOTATION 은 "DON'T WORRY , WE CAN SUPPORT YOU" 라고 언급한것임을 참고바람. 건승기원함. 끝

국기국

PAGE 1

공   란

공   란

공   란

공 란

공　　　　　란

공   란

공   란

남북한 유엔 가입 총회결안 추진 및 기본입장 각서

공 란

공 란

공   란

공　　　란

공   란

공   란

공   란

공 란

공 란

공　　　란

관리번호 91-1091

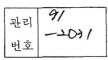

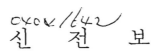발   신   전   보

번   호 : WUN-0741   910403 2202 DQ 차별급 ㉠급

수   신 : 주 유연, 미   대사. 총영사//

발   신 : 장   관   (국연)

제   목 : 유엔가입 추진 (메모랜덤)

대 : UNW-0767, 68, 69

대호 메모랜덤안을 일부 자구 수정하여 별첨 타전하니 아래와 같이 조치하고
그 결과 보고바람.

1. 미국포함 CG 회원국에게 협의하는 형식으로 동 메모랜덤을 사전에
   개별 전달바람.

2. 중국, 소련에 대하여는 상기 핵심우방국에 대한 조치를 필한후 귀대표부에서
   안보리문서로 배포 요청하기전 상기 메모랜덤 제출사실 및 동 개요를
   구두로 설명하기 바람. (안보리 문서 배포요청 서한발송과 동시에
   동 메모랜덤을 전달하는 것은 무방하다고 봄.)

3. 본부로서는 메모랜덤을 가급적 조속 안보리문서로 회람시키는 것이
   좋을 것으로 판단하고 있는 바, 귀대표부의 안보리문서 배포요청
   서한발송 일시는 정해지는 대로 사전 보고바람.

4. 각서제출에 따른 아국특파원 및 주재국언론등을 대상으로 하는 홍보
   계획 보고바람.

첨 부 : 메모랜덤 1부.   끝. 검토필:91.6.30|

예 고 : 1991.12.31. 고 일반   (국제기구조약국장   문동석)

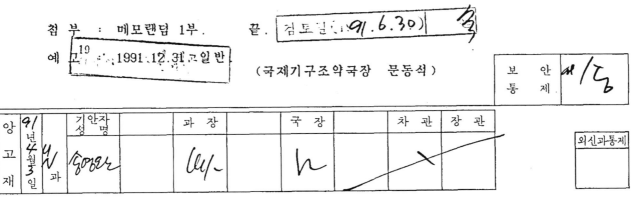

보 안 통 제 : 제/급

외신과통제

0033

MEMORANDUM OF THE GOVERNMENT OF THE REPUBLIC OF KOREA

The Government of the Republic of Korea has made clear on previous occasions its position concerning membership of the Republic of Korea in the United Nations, particularly its determination to seek United Nations membership during the course of this year.

The Republic of Korea, as a peace-loving state willing and able to carry out all obligations set forth in the United Nations Charter, is fully qualified for membership in the United Nations. As a country which maintains almost universal diplomatic relations and as the world's twelfth largest trading nation, it is ready to make its due contribution to the work of the United Nations as a full Member and in a manner commensurate with its standing in the international community.

The principle of universality cherished by the United Nations requires the admission of all eligible sovereign states that wish to join the United Nations. This principle gains more relevance than ever as the United Nations assumes an increasingly vital role in the post-Cold War era. The unprecedented changes taking place in the international political environment, featuring a new spirit of reconciliation and cooperation, call for the resolution of Korea's membership question at long last.

As was eloquently manifested last year during the general debate of the 45th session of the General Assembly, it has become the sense of the international community that the admission of the Republic of Korea to United Nations membership should be realized without further delay.

0034

In seeking United Nations membership, the Republic of Korea reiterates its earnest hope that the Democratic People's Republic of Korea (DPRK) will also join the United Nations, either together with the South, or at the time the North deems appropriate. The Republic of Korea restates its position that it would welcome DPRK's membership.

Furthermore, the Republic of Korea holds the view that the parallel membership of both Koreas in the United Nations is entirely without prejudice to the ultimate objective of Korea's reunification. Parallel membership should constitute a powerful confidence building measure insofar as it will represent a firm commitment of both Koreas to the provisions and principles of the United Nations Charter.

The unification of East and West Germany and of North and South Yemen, each of which had maintained separate membership in the United Nations, validates this view and disproves the contention that United Nations membership might serve to perpetuate or legitimize Korea's national division, thus hindering efforts for Korea's reunification.

It is a matter of fact that the international community has long recognized the existence of South and North Korea on the Korean Peninsula. In reality, the Republic of Korea and the DPRK maintain diplomatic relations with 146 and 105 countries respectively. Ninety of these countries maintain concurrent diplomatic relations with both. Each also has separate membership in most inter-governmental organizations, including specialized agencies of the United Nations. Thus, Korea's United Nations membership, separate or simultaneous, will be a logical corollary of the international political reality.

0035

In the sincere belief that United Nations membership will contribute to the process of Korean reconciliation and reunification, as well as enhance peace and security on the Korean Peninsula, the Republic of Korea has made every effort in good faith to join the ~~UN~~ United Nations together with the DPRK during the course of last year, but without success.

Despite these efforts, however, the DPRK has adhered to the "single-seat membership" formula which is not only infeasible but runs counter to the provisions of the United Nations Charter and the practices followed by the United Nations and its specialized agencies. The lack of support from the United Nations Member States with respect to this formula during the general debate last year reflects their disapproval of the North Korean formula.

The Government of the Republic of Korea remains hopeful of realizing membership of both Koreas during the course of this year. However, if the DPRK continues to oppose this option and for any reason choose not to join the United Nations, the Republic of Korea, exercising its sovereign right, will take the necessary step toward its membership before the opening of the 46th session of the General Assembly.

The Government of the Republic of Korea is convinced that, with the overwhelming support of the Member States of the United Nations for the legitimate cause of its membership, the Republic of Korea will be able to assume its rightful place in the United Nations in the months ahead.

0036

외 무 부

관리번호 91 -2055

종 별 : 긴 급

번 호 : UNW-0786

일 시 : 91 0403 2000

수 신 : 장관(국연)

발 신 : 주 유엔 대사

제 목 : 유엔가입 추진(메모랜덤)

대:WUN-0741 (1), 0680 (2)

연:UNW-0765

1. 대호 관련 당관 조치계획을 아래보고함.

가. 미국에 대하여는 4.4. 한.미 대사간 조찬협의시 대호 메모랜덤 전달및관련사항을 설명하고, 여타 CG 국가에 대하여도 4.4. 중 개별적으로 전달함.

나. 안보리 문서로 배포요청 서한은 4.5. 12:30 본직이 직접 안보리의장을 방문, 수교예정임.

다. 중국, 소련에 대하여는 4.4. 또는 4.5. 중 관계관과 접촉, 아측각서 사본을 전달예정임.

라. 유엔주재 특파원에 대하여는 4.5. 안보리의장 방문직후 본직주재 오찬시, 아국특파원에 대하여는 4.5. 오후 별도로 금번 각서 사본을 배포하면서 관련사항을 설명하되, 안보리문서 배포시기(4.5. 오전 제출시 4.8. 오후내지 4.9. 중배포예상), 중국대표부가 본국정부에 보고하는데 소요되는 시간(특히 아국문서배포후 외교부 대변인의 정례 브리핑시 언급 가능성등 감안), 국내홍보 효과제고를 위한 주말회피 필요성등을 감안하여, 서울시간 4.8.(월) 보도토록 조치코자함.(4.7. 까지 EMBARGO)

2. 우방 안보리 비상임이사국 및 주요 유엔회원국에 대하여도 상기 각서배포전에 직접 전달코자 하는바 대호(2) 관련 본부에서 직접 조치하고자 하는 사항이 있는지 여부 회시바람. (?)

3. 대호 본부 수정안중 아래 부분만 수정, 시행코자 하는바, 본부의견 긴급회시바람.

가.3 항 (THE PRINCIPLE OF UNIVERSALITY ...) 초반의 "ALL ELIGIBLE SOVEREIGN STATES THAT WISH" 는 당관안대로 "ANY... STATE...WISHES " 로 함.

국기국   장관   차관   1차보   정와대   안기부

나. 마지막에서 4 번째항 (IN THE SINCERE BELIEF...) 중 "ROK HAS MADE...TO JOIN THE UN TOGETHER WITH THE DPRK" 는 당관안대로 "ROK HAS MADE ...TO PERSUADE THE DPRK TO ACCEPT PARALLEL MEMBERSHIP OF BOTH KOREAS IN THE UN" 으로 하고, "LAST YEAR " 는 "THE LAST YEAR " 로 함.

(이유: 본부 의도와 실제 영어표현이 의미상의 차이가 있음. 즉 본부수정안은 아국이 북한과 함께 작년중 가입노력을 했으나 실패한것으로 해석됨."THE LAST YEAR " 는 현재까지의 1 년을 의미).

다. 마지막에서 3 번째항 (DESPITE...)의 "INFEASIBLE " 은 당관안대로 "UNWORKABLE " 로 함.

(이유:INFEASIBLE 은 실제 잘 사용되지 않으며, UNWORKABLE 은 INFEASIBLE 을 포함하여 보다 광범위한 의미). 끝

(대사 노창희-국장)

예고:91.12.31. 일반

접수번호 91.6.30

PAGE 2

0038

	분류번호	보존기간

발 신 전 보

수   신 :   주 유엔   대사. /총영사/

발   신 :   장관 (국연)

제   목 :   유연가입 추진 (메모랜덤)

대 : UNW-0786

연 : WUN-0741

1. 대호, 각서내용 관련, 연호 본부 타전한 내용대로 시행바람.

2. 대호 2항관련, 안보리이사국 15개국중 4개 핵심우방국(미,영,불,

벨지움) 및 3개 미수교국(중국, 쿠바, 짐바브웨) 그리고 실무교섭단이 이미

파견된 에쿠아돌은 제외하고, 7개국(오지리, 인도, 예멘, 자이르, 코트디봐르,

루마니아, 소련)에 대하여만 본직명의 친서를 발송할 계획임.

3. 상기 친서 발송은 귀관에서 아측 각서를 안보리문서로 배포 요청한

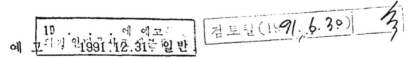

직후 각국 수도에서 전달토록 할 예정인 바, 귀지에서의 CG 회원국 및 중국, 소련

그리고 주요 유엔회원국에 대한 아측 각서전달은 대호대로 시행바람.

4. 본부에서도 4.8. 10:00까지 Embargo 하여 아측 각서 배포사실 및

동 개요를 대언론 발표 예정임. 끝.

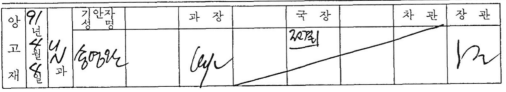

예 고 : 1991 . 12 . 31 . 일반   검토필(1991.6.30)

(국제기구조약국장 문동석)

	보 안 통 제	

앙 고 재	91년 4월 8일	기안자 성명	과 장	국 장	차 관	장 관

외신과통제

0039

공   란

발 신 전 보

번 호 : WUN-0755   910404 1932 FG   종별 : 지급

수 신 : 주   유엔   대사♣♣♧♣♣♧사 (서대원 참사관님)

발 신 : 장 관   (이규형 배상)

제 목 : 메모랜덤

연 : WUN-0741

1. 연호 메모랜덤 내용에서 사용하고 있는 북한 표기는 그대로 사용해 주시기 바랍니다. 즉 PARA 5의 두째줄에서는 Democratic People's Republic of Korea(DPRK)로 적었고, 나머지 PARA 5의 마지막줄, PARA 8, PARA 10, PARA 11에 사용한 것은 전부 the DPRK로 하였으니 유의하여 주시기 바랍니다.
그대로 동기하도록

2. 건안하시기 기원하오며.   끝.

예   예. 그 문에   표8 : 독후꽈기   ⁄з

보 안 통 제	山/

앙고재	년월일	유엔과	기안자 성명	과 장	국 장	차 관	장 관	외신과통제
				山/			山	

0041

원 본

외 무 부

종 별 : 지 급

번 호 : UNW-0796

일 시 : 91 0404 1730

수 신 : 장관(국연)

발 신 : 주 유엔 대사

제 목 : 유엔가입추진(메모랜덤)

대:WUN-0750

연:UNW-0786

연호 4.5. 아국특파원 브리핑 및 주유엔 외국 특파원 오찬시(별첨 참석자 명단 참조) 참고코자 하니, 대호 4 항 관련 본부에서 작성중인 보도자료가 있으면 당관에 타전내지 FAX 송부 바람. 끝

첨부:상기 오찬참석자 명단:UNW(F)-151

(대사 노창희-국장)

검토필(91.6.30)

국기국

91.04.05   07:47
외신 2과   통제관 CF

0042

UNW(F)-151 10404 1730
(국연)

총 1 대

Guest List hosted by Amb. Chang Hee ROE
for Senior Correspondents of UNCA
at 13:00 on Friday, 05 April 1991
at UNDDR (Private Dining Room)

A F P	Mr. Bruno FRANCESCHI
A P	Ms. Victoria GRAHAM
Reuters	Mr. Anthony GOODMAN
U P I	Mr. Tuyet NGUYEN
TASS	Mr. Evgueni MENKES
Xinhua	Mr. Wenrong QIAN
Kyodo	Mr. Hiroshi OSHIMA
D P A	Mr. Gerd-Eckard ZEHM
Tanjug	Mr. Vladimir HOLOVKA
USIA	Ms. Judith AITA
Yonhap	Mr. Jeon-Seon ROH
N Y T	Mr. Paul LEWIS
FEER/C S M	Mr. Ted MORELLO
A B C	Mr. Tom OSBORNE
B B C	Mr. Chris GUNNES

별첨

/ ― /

0043

MEMORANDUM OF THE GOVERNMENT OF THE REPUBLIC OF KOREA

5 April 1991

The Government of the Republic of Korea has made clear on previous occasions its position concerning membership of the Republic of Korea in the United Nations, particularly its determination to seek United Nations membership during the course of this year.

The Republic of Korea, as a peace-loving state willing and able to carry out all obligations set forth in the United Nations Charter, is fully qualified for membership in the United Nations. As a country which maintains almost universal diplomatic relations and as the world's twelfth largest trading nation, it is ready to make its due contribution to the work of the United Nations as a full Member and in a manner commensurate with its standing in the international community.

The principle of universality cherished by the United Nations requires the admission of all eligible sovereign states that wish to join the United Nations. This principle gains more relevance than ever as the United Nations assumes an increasingly vital role in the post-Cold War era. The unprecedented changes taking place in the international political environment, featuring a new spirit of reconciliation and cooperation, call for the resolution of Korea's membership question at long last.

As was eloquently manifested last year during the general debate of the 45th session of the General Assembly, it has become the sense of the international community that the admission of the Republic of Korea to United Nations membership should be realized without further delay.

/...

-1-

0044

In seeking United Nations membership, the Republic of Korea reiterates its earnest hope that the Democratic People's Republic of Korea(DPRK) will also join the United Nations, either together with the South, or at the time the North deems appropriate. The Republic of Korea restates its position that it would welcome DPRK's membership.

Furthermore, the Republic of Korea holds the view that the parallel membership of both Koreas in the United Nations is entirely without prejudice to the ultimate objective of Korea's reunification. Parallel membership should constitute a powerful confidence building measure insofar as it will represent a firm commitment of both Koreas to the provisions and principles of the United Nations Charter.

The unification of East and West Germany and of North and South Yemen, each of which had maintained separate membership in the United Nations, validates this view and disproves the contention that United Nations membership might serve to perpetuate or legitimize Korea's national division, thus hindering efforts for Korea's reunification.

It is a matter of fact that the international community has long recognized the existence of South and North Korea on the Korean Peninsula. In reality, the Republic of Korea and the DPRK maintain diplomatic relations with 146 and 105 countries respectively. Ninety of these countries maintain concurrent diplomatic relations with both. Each also has separate membership in most inter-governmental organizations, including specialized agencies of the United Nations. Thus, Korea's United Nations membership, separate or simultaneous, will be a logical corollary of the international political reality.

/...

-2-

0045

In the sincere belief that United Nations membership will contribute to the process of Korean reconciliation and reunification, as well as enhance peace and security on the Korean Peninsula, the Republic of Korea has made every effort in good faith to join the United Nations together with the DPRK during the course of last year, but without success.

Despite these efforts, however, the DPRK has adhered to the 'single-seat membership' formula which is not only infeasible but runs counter to the provisions of the United Nations Charter and the practices followed by the United Nations and its specialized agenices. The lack of support from the United Nations Member States with respect to this formula during the general debate last year reflects their disapproval of the North Korean formula.

The Government of the Republic of Korea remains hopeful of realizing membership of both Koreas during the course of this year. However, if the DPRK continues to oppose this option and for any reason chooses not to join the United Nations, the Republic of Korea, exercising its sovereign right, will take the necessary step toward its membership before the opening of the 46th session of the General Assembly.

The Government of the Republic of Korea is convinced that, with the overwhelming support of the Member States of the United Nations for the legitimate cause of its membership, the Republic of Korea will be able to assume its rightful place in the United Nations in the months ahead.

- - - - -

-3-

발 신 전 보

번 호 : WUN-0767   910405 1806 FL 종별 : 지급

수 신 : 주 유엔   대사.//총영사

발 신 : 장 관 (국연)

제 목 : 유엔가입 추진 (메모랜덤)

대 : UNW-0796, 0786

연 : WUN-0750

1. 대호, 아국정부 각서 배포에 관한 보도자료를 별첨 타전하니 참고바람.
(별첨 내용은 국내홍보 차원에서 남북한 동시가입 및 앞으로도 동시가입을 위해
우리가 노력할 것임을 강조한 측면이 있음을 감안하기 바람.)

2. 대호 특히 외국 특파원 접촉시 동 보도자료가 국내에서 4.8.(월)이후에
보도될 것임을 감안 4.7(뉴욕시간)까지 embargo를 지켜줄 것을 당부바람.

첨 부 : 보도자료 1부. 끝.
예 고 : 19 . . 에 예고 대기 1991. 12. 31. 분일 반

(국제기구조약국장   문동석)

검토필(91.6.30)

보 안 통 제	내

앙 고 재	91 년 4 월 5 일	기안자 성명		과 장		국 장		차 관	장 관		외신과통제

0047

보 도 자 료
외 무 부

제   호   문의전화 : 720-2408~10   보도일시 : 1991. 4. 8. 10:00시

제   목 : 유연가입문제에 관한 각서

가 . 정부는 '금일 유연가입 문제에 관한 우리의 입장을 종합적으로 설명하고
   특히 금년중 유연가입을 실현하고자 하는 의지를 밝히는 91.4.5.자 각서를
   발표하였다.

나 . 노창희 주유연대사는 1991.4.5. 유연안전보장이사회 의장인 주유연 "노텔담"
   벨지움대사를 방문, 동 각서가 유연안전보장이사회 문서로서 배포되도록
   요청하였고, 이에 따라 동 각서는 안보리 문서로서 금주초 유연에서 유연
   회원국 및 산하기구에 배포될 예정이다.

다 . 정부는 동 각서에서 북한도 우리와 함께 유연에 가입하여 유연의 활동에
   적극 기여해야 할 것임을 강조하고, 남북한이 유연에 각각 회원국으로서
   가입할 경우 남북한은 유연헌장의 의무와 원칙을 수락하게 되므로 이는
   남북한 상호간의 강력한 신뢰구축 방안이 될 것을 강조하였다.

다 . 동 각서는 그간 정부가 북한과 함께 유연에 가입하기 위하여 최선의 노력을
   경주하여 왔으나 별 성과가 없었음에 유감을 표시하였으며, 특히 북한측의
   소위 단일의석 가입안이 45차 유연총회에서 입증된 바와 같이 국제사회의
   지지가 전혀없고 실현불가능한 제안임을 다시한번 지적하였다.

라 . 끝으로 정부는 동 각서에서 앞으로 북한과 함께 유연에 가입하기 위한 노력을
   계속할 것이나, 북한이 우리의 노력에 호응해 오지 않을 경우 금년 제46차
   유연총회가 개막(91.9.17)되기전 유연가입을 위한 필요한 조치를 취할 것임을
   천명하였다.

첨 부 : 유연가입문제에 관한 대한민국정부 각서 1부.

0048

관리 번호	9/ — 2|12

외 무 부

종 별 :

번 호 : UNW-0815
일 시 : 91 0405 1640

수 신 : 장관 (국연,해신,기정)

발 신 : 주 유엔 대사

제 목 : 유엔가입 추진 (메모랜덤)

대: WUN-0741,0767

연: UNW-0796,0786

1. 본직은 4.5. 오전 아국특파원 (9 명) 대상 브리핑 실시후 AP, NYT 등 유엔 주요 외신기자 (12 명) 대상 오찬 간담을 갖고 대호 아국정부 각서 안보리 제출 관련 설명 (본부 보도자료 및 영문각서 배포)후 질의응답을 가졌음.

2. 주요 질문요지는 가입신청 시기, 예상되는 중국태도, 북한입장의 변화 가능성 여부 등에 주관심을 보였음.

3. 동 간담에 참석한 중국 신화사통신 특파원 YANG YUEHUA 는 우선 외무성등 정부내 주요 인사에게 배포하는 참고 통신자료로 송고예정이며 대외 배포여부는 본사에서 결정될것 이라함.

4. 동지 아국 특파원 송고관련 EMBARGO 시간을 준수해 주도록 요청하였으나본부에서 재 협조토록 배려바람. 끝

(대사 노창희-국장, 관장)

예고:91.12.31. 일반
의거 일반문서로 재분류

검토필(1991.6.30)

국기국	장관	차관	1차보	정문국	청와대	안기부	공보처

공   란

원 본

외 무 부

종　별 : 지 급

번　호 : UNW-0822　　　　　　　　　일　시 : 91 0405 2030

수　신 : 장관(국연)

발　신 : 주 유엔 대사

제　목 : 유엔가입추진(메모랜덤)

연:UNW-0786

대:WUN-0741,0750

1. 대호 아국정부의 메모랜덤을 본직명의 서한에 첨부, 금 4.5. 오후 안보리
의장에게 전달하였음.

2. 안보리 사무국 CHAN 담당관에 의하면 아국각서가 빠르면 4.8(월) 오후
안보리문서로 배포될 수 있을것이라고함. 끝

(대사 노창희-국장)

검토필(1991. 6. 30)

국기국　　장관　　차관　　1차보　　청와대　　안기부

	분류번호	보존기간

관리	91
번호	— 2102

발 신 전 보

WHG-0328 910406 1600 DU
WEM-0889 910406 1559 DU

종별 :

수 신 : 주 EM 대사. /총영사/ (사본 : 주유엔대사)

WPD-0329 WYG-0298
WRM-0258 WSV-1021
WBL-0213 WCZ-0260

발 신 : 장 관 (국연)

제 목 : 유연가입관련 정부각서 배포

1. 본부는 금년도 우리의 유연가입 추진과 관련 정부의 기본입장을 밝히는 메모랜덤을 유연 안보리문서로 배포코자 조치중이며, 4.8일경 회람될 예정임.

2. 동 메모랜덤의 주요내용은 아래와 같은 바(영문(전문)은 안보리문서로 배포와 동시 평문 타전 예정임), 귀관에서는 주재국 요로와 접촉 동 메모랜덤을 수고, 우리의 입장을 설명하고 결과 보고바람.

ㅇ 연내 유연가입 실현의지 천명

ㅇ 아국가입의 당위성 및 여건 성숙

    - 평화애호국으로서 유연가입 자격 충분

    - 국제사회내 위상에 상응하는 기여 의지

    - 아국의 가입이 더이상 지체되어서는 안된다는 것이 국제사회내 공통된 인식

ㅇ 동시가입 문제에 관한 아국입장

    - ~~의 가입을 반대치 않으며, 오히려~~ 북한의 가입을 환영함.

    - 남북한의 유연가입은 궁극적 통일목표에 장애가 되지 않으며, 오히려 남북한간 화해와 통일에 기여함.

ㅇ 북한측이 계속 반대할 경우, 금년 제 46차 총회 개막이전 우리만의 가입을 위한 필요 조치 예정

보 안 통 제	서명

앙 고 재	91 년 4 월 5 일 유 엔 과	기안 책임자 성명		과 장	국 장	차관	차 관	장 관
				서명	서명			

외신과통제

0052

3. 앞으로 귀주재국이 적절한 계기에 우리의 유엔가입 입장에 대한 지지 입장을 공개적으로 밝혀주는 것이 북한의 태도변화 및 중국의 대북한 설득노력을 촉진시킬 것으로 사료되는 바, 가능한한 공개적인 지지입장 확보에 노력바람.

끝.

(차관 유종하)

예고문: 1991년 12월 31. 일반.

검토필(91 . 6 . 30)

0053

長官報告事項

1991. 4. 5.

國際機構條約局
國際聯合課 (16)

報告畢

題目 : 유엔加入에 관한 메모랜덤 配布

내주초(4.8 또는 4.9) 安保理文書로 配布될 豫定인 유엔加入에 관한 메모랜덤의 主要友邦國等에 대한 事前 傳達 및 對言論 弘報計劃을 아래와 같이 報告드립니다.

---

1. 駐유엔 代表部 措置計劃

가. 覺書의 安保理文書 配布要請

○ 4.5(金) 12:30 駐유엔大使가 安保理議長(벨지음 大使)에게 直接 配布要請書翰 傳達

나. 核心友邦國

○ 美國 : 4.4(木) 韓.美 駐유엔大使間 朝餐 協議時 메모랜덤 說明 및 傳達

○ 餘他 核心友邦國(영.불.일.카.벨지음) : 4.4(木)중 個別 接觸, 傳達

다. 中國 및 蘇聯

○ 4.4(木) 또는 4.5(金) 關係官 接觸, 覺書發表 趣旨說明 및 覺書傳達

※ 각 실국에도 협조처e
행할것. ㉛

0054

라. 其他 安保理 非常任理事國 및 主要 유엔會員國

　　º 메모랜덤이 安保理文書로 配布되기 이전 直接 傳達

마. 對言論 弘報 (뉴욕시간 4.7(日)까지 Embargo 前提)

　　º 유엔駐在 外國特派員 : 4.5(金) 駐유엔大使가 安保理議長 訪問직후
　　　特派員과의 午餐時 我國立場 說明 및 메모랜덤 사본 傳達

　　º 我國特派員 : 4.5(金) 午後 別添 報道資料를 基本으로하여
　　　브리핑 實施 및 메모랜덤 사본 傳達

2. 本部 措置計劃

(가) 長官 親書 發送

　　º 對 象 : 유엔事務總長 및 安保理理事國 7個國 (오지리, 인도,
　　　　　　　　　예맨, 자이르, 코트디브와르, 루마니아, 소련)

　　※ 安保理理事國中 核心友邦國 4個國 (미, 영, 불, 벨지움) 및
　　　未修交 3個國 (중국, 쿠바, 짐바브웨)과 實務交涉團 旣派遣國
　　　(에쿠아돌)은 親書 發送 對象에서 除外

　　º 上記 親書는 各國 首都에서 傳達 (유엔사무총장 앞 친서는 뉴욕에서 전달)

(나) 駐韓 公館에 대한 回覽公翰 發送

　　º 4.8(月)字 全 駐韓公館 앞 回覽公翰에 메모랜덤을 添付하여 送付豫定

(다) 國內弘報

　　º 言論機關에 4.8(月) 10:00까지 Embargo 措置하여 別添 報道資料 配布

　　º 메모랜덤 內容을 중심으로 하여 "外交問題 解說"資料를 作成, DM망을
　　　통해 配布

添 附 : 報道資料 (案) 1부. 　　끝.

0055

보 도 자 료
의 무 부

제   호   문의전화 : 720-2408~10   보도일시 : 91 . 4 . 8 . 10:00 시

제   목 : 유연가입문제에 관한 각서

가. 정부는 금일 유연가입 문제에 관한 우리의 입장을 종합적으로 설명하고
    특히 금년중 유연가입을 실현하고자 하는 의지를 밝히는 91.4.5.자 각서를
    발표하였다.

나. 노창희 주유엔대사는 1991.4.5. 유엔안전보장이사회 의장인 주유엔 "노텔담"
    벨지움대사를 방문, 동 각서가 유엔안전보장이사회 문서로서 배포되도록
    요청하였고, 이에 따라 동 각서는 안보리 문서로서 금주초 유연에서 유연
    회원국 및 산하기구에 배포될 예정이다.

다. 정부는 동 각서에서 북한도 우리와 함께 유연에 가입하여 유연의 활동에
    적극 기여해야 할 것임을 강조하고, 남북한이 유연에 각각 회원국으로서
    가입할 경우 남북한은 유연헌장의 의무와 원칙을 수락하게 되므로 이는
    남북한 상호간의 강력한 신뢰구축 방안이 될 것임을 강조하였다.

라. 동 각서는 그간 정부가 북한과 함께 유연에 가입하기 위하여 최선의 노력을
    경주하여 왔으나 별 성과가 없었음에 유감을 표시하였으며, 특히 북한측의
    소위 단일의석 가입안이 제45차 유연총회에서 입증된 바와 같이 국제사회의
    지지가 전혀없고 실현불가능한 제안임을 다시한번 지적하였다.

마. 끝으로 정부는 동 각서에서 앞으로 북한과 함께 유연에 가입하기 위한 노력을
    계속할 것이나, 북한이 우리의 노력에 호응해 오지 않을 경우 금년 제46차
    유연총회가 개막(91.9.17)되기전 유연가입을 위한 필요한 조치를 취할 것임을
    천명하였다.

첨 부 : 유연가입문제에 관한 대한민국정부 각서 1부.

0056

長 官 報 告 事 項

報 告 畢

1991. 4. 6

國際機構條約局
國際聯合課 (16)

題目 : 유엔加入에 관한 메모랜덤 配布

내주초(4.8 또는 4.9) 安保理文書로 配布될 豫定인 유엔加入에 관한
메모랜덤의 主要友邦國等에 대한 事前 傳達 및 對言論 弘報計劃을 아래와
같이 報告드립니다.

1. 駐유엔 代表部 措置計劃

가. 覺書의 安保理文書 配布要請

  ° 4.5(金) 12:30 駐유엔大使가 安保理議長(벨지움 대사)에게 直接
    配布要請書翰 傳達

나. 核心友邦國

  ° 美國 : 4.4(木) 韓.美 駐유엔大使間 朝餐 協議時 메모랜덤 說明
    및 傳達

  ° 餘他 核心友邦國(영, 불, 일, 카, 벨지움) : 4.4(木)중 個別
                 接觸, 傳達

공	담 당	과 장	국 장	차 관 보	차 관	장 관
람						

0057

다. 中國 및 蘇聯

　　ㅇ 4.4(木) 또는 4.5(金) 關係官 接觸, 覺書發表 趣旨說明 및 覺書傳達

라. 其他 安保理 非常任理事國 및 主要 유엔會員國

　　ㅇ 메모랜덤이 安保理文書로 配布되기 이전 直接 傳達

마. 對言論 弘報 (뉴욕시간 4.7(日)까지 Embargo 前提)

　　ㅇ 유엔駐在 外國特派員 : 4.5(金) 駐유엔大使가 安保理議長 訪問직후
　　　　特派員과의 午餐時 我國立場 說明 및 메모랜덤 사본 傳達

　　ㅇ 我國特派員 : 4.5(金) 午後 別添 報道資料를 基本으로하여
　　　　브리핑 實施 및 메모랜덤 사본 傳達

2. 本部 措置計劃

가. 長官 親書 發送

　　ㅇ 對　象 : 유엔事務總長 및 安保理理事國 7個國 (오지리, 인도,
　　　　　　　　　　　예멘, 자이르, 코트디브와르, 루마니아, 소련)

　　※ 安保理理事國中 核心友邦國 4個國 (미, 영, 불, 벨지음) 및
　　　未修交 3個國 (중국, 쿠바, 짐바브웨)과 實務交涉團 旣派遣國
　　　(에쿠아돌)은 親書 發送 對象에서 除外

　　ㅇ 上記 親書는 各國 首都에서 傳達(유엔사무총장 앞 친서는 뉴욕에서 전달)

나. 駐韓 公館에 대한 回覽公翰 發送

　　ㅇ 4.8(月)字 全 駐韓公館 앞 回覽公翰에 메모랜덤을 添付하여 送付豫定

다. 國內弘報

　　ㅇ 言論機關에 4.8(月) 10:00까지 Embargo 措置하여 別添 報道資料 配布

　　ㅇ 메모랜덤 內容을 중심으로 "外交問題 解說" 資料를 作成, DM망을 통해 配布

添附 : 報道資料 (案)1부. 　 끝.

0058

보 도 자 료
의 무 부

제   호   문의전화 : 720-2405~10   보도일시 : 91 . 4 . 8 . 10:00 시

제 목 : 유연가입문제에 관한 각서

가. 정부는 금일 유연가입 문제에 관한 우리의 입장을 종합적으로 설명하고
   특히 금년중 유연가입을 실현하고자 하는 의지를 밝히는 91.4.5.자 각서를
   발표하였다.

나. 노창희 주유연대사는 1991.4.5. 유연안전보장이사희 의장인 주유연 "노텔담"
   벨지음대사를 방문. 동 각서가 유연안전보장이사희 문서로서 배포되도록
   요청하였고. 이에 따라 등 각서는 안보리 문서로서 금주초 유연에서 유연
   회원국 및 산하기구에 배포될 예정이다.

다. 정부는 동 각서에서 북한도 우리와 함께 유연에 가입하여 유연의 활동에
   적극 기여해야 할 것임을 강조하고. 남북한이 유연에 각각 회원국으로서
   가입할 경우 남북한은 유연현장의 의무와 원칙을 수락하게 되므로 이는
   남북한 상호간의 강력한 신뢰구축 방안이 될 것임을 강조하였다.

라. 동 각서는 그간 정부가 북한과 함께 유연에 가입하기 위하여 최선의 노력을
   경주하여 왔으나 별 성과가 없었음에 유감을 표시하였으며. 특히 북한측의
   소위 단일의석 가입안이 제45차 유연총회에서 입증된 바와 같이 국제사회의
   지지가 전혀없고 실현불가능한 제안임을 다시한번 지적하였다.

마. 끝으로 정부는 동 각서에서 앞으로 북한과 함께 유연에 가입하기 위한 노력을
   계속할 것이나. 북한이 우리의 노력에 호응해 오지 않을 경우 금년 제46차
   유연총회가 개막(91.9.17)되기전 유연가입을 위한 필요한 조치를 취할 것임을
   천명하였다.

첨 부 : 유연가입문제에 관한 대한민국정부 각서 1부.   0059

공　　　란

남북한 유엔 가입 총회결안 추진 및 기본입장 각서

발 신 전 보

	분류번호	보존기간

번 호 : EM-0011   910407 1459   DU   종별 :

수 신 : 주 EM 대사. 총영사

발 신 : 장 관 (국연)

제 목 : 정부각서 타전

유엔가입문제에 관한 정부각서 별첨 타전함.

첨부 : 동각서 (영문) 1부. 끝.

(국제기구조약국장 문동석)

		보 안 통 제	ᄴ

앙고재	91년 4월 7일	기안 성명	유연과 홍	과 장 ᄴ	국 장 전결	차 관	장 관	외신과통제

OGO 91-233

The Ministry of Foreign Affairs presents its compliments to all Diplomatic and Consular Missions and has the honour to enclose herewith a memorandum of the Government of the Republic of Korea concerning its United Nations membership.

In presenting the memorandum, Ministry of Foreign Affairs wishes to draw the attention of all Diplomatic and Consular Missions on the position of the Government of the Republic of Korea, particularly its determination to seek United Nations membership before the opening of the 46th session of the General Assembly of the United Nations. In this connection, the Government of the Republic of Korea respectfully requests all Member States of the United Nations, especially those represented in the Republic of Korea, to render their valuable support for the realization of its admission to United Nations membership.

The Memorandum will be circulated as an official document of the United Nations Security Council.

The Ministry of Foreign Affairs avails itself of this opportunity to renew to all Diplomatic and Consular Missions the assurances of its highest consideration.

Enclosure : as stated.

Seoul, 8 April 1991

0062

MINISTRY OF FOREIGN AFFAIRS
REPUBLIC OF KOREA

OGO 91- 233

The Ministry of Foreign Affairs presents its compliments to all
Diplomatic and Consular Missions and has the honour to enclose herewith
a memorandum of the Government of the Republic of Korea concerning its
United Nations membership.

In presenting the memorandum, Ministry of Foreign Affairs wishes to
draw the attention of all Diplomatic and Consular Missions on the position
of the Government of the Republic of Korea, particularly its determination
to seek United Nations membership before the opening of the 46th session
of the General Assembly of the United Nations. In this connection, the
Government of the Republic of Korea respectfully requests all Member States
of the United Nations, especially those represented in the Republic of Korea,
to render their valuable support for the realization of its admission to United
Nations membership.

The Memorandum will be circulated as an official document of the
United Nations Security Council.

The Ministry of Foreign Affairs avails itself of this opportunity
to renew to all Diplomatic and Consular Missions the assurances of its
highest consideration.

Enclosure : as stated.

Seoul, 8 April 1991

0063

MINISTRY OF FOREIGN AFFAIRS
REPUBLIC OF KOREA

OGO 91- 233

The Ministry of Foreign Affairs presents its compliments to all Diplomatic and Consular Missions and has the honour to enclose herewith a memorandum of the Government of the Republic of Korea concerning its United Nations membership.

In presenting the memorandum, Ministry of Foreign Affairs wishes to draw the attention of all Diplomatic and Consular Missions on the position of the Government of the Republic of Korea, particularly its determination to seek United Nations membership before the opening of the 46th session of the General Assembly of the United Nations. In this connection, the Government of the Republic of Korea respectfully requests all Member States of the United Nations, especially those represented in the Republic of Korea, to render their valuable support for the realization of its admission to United Nations membership.

The Memorandum will be circulated as an official document of the United Nations Security Council.

The Ministry of Foreign Affairs avails itself of this opportunity to renew to all Diplomatic and Consular Missions the assurances of its highest consideration.

Enclosure : as stated.

Seoul, 8 April 1991

0064

보 도 자 료

외 무 부

제   호   문의전화 : 720-2408~10   보도일시 : 91 . 4 . 8 . 10 :00 시

제 목 : 유엔가입문제에 관한 각서

가. 정부는 금일 유엔가입 문제에 관한 우리의 입장을 종합적으로 설명하고
   특히 금년중 유엔가입을 실현하고자 하는 의지를 밝히는 91.4.5.자 각서를
   발표하였다.

나. 노창희 주유엔대사는 1991.4.5. 유엔안전보장이사회 의장인 주유엔 "노텔담"
   벨지움대사를 방문, 동 각서가 유엔안전보장이사회 문서로서 배포되도록
   요청하였고, 이에 따라 동 각서는 안보리 문서로서 금주초 유엔에서 유엔
   회원국 및 산하기구에 배포될 예정이다.

다. 정부는 동 각서에서 북한도 우리와 함께 유엔에 가입하여 유엔의 활동에
   적극 기여하여 주기를 바란다는 우리의 입장을 다시 천명하고, 남북한이
   유엔에 각각 회원국으로서 가입할 경우 남북한은 유엔헌장의 의무와 원칙을
   수락하게 되므로 이는 남북한 상호간의 강력한 신뢰구축 방안의 하나가 될
   것임을 강조하였다.

라. 동 각서는 그간 정부가 북한과 함께 유엔에 가입하기 위하여 최선의 노력을
   경주하여 왔으나 별 성과가 없었음에 유감을 표시하였으며, 특히 북한측의
   소위 단일의석 가입안이 제 45차 유엔총회에서 입증된 바와 같이 국제사회의
   지지가 전혀없고 실현불가능한 제안임을 다시한번 지적하였다.

마. 끝으로 정부는 동 각서에서 앞으로 북한과 함께 유엔에 가입하기 위한 노력을
   계속할 것이나, 북한이 우리의 노력에 호응해 오지 않을 경우 금년 제46차
   유엔총회가 개막(91.9.17)되기전 유엔가입을 위한 필요한 조치를 취할 것임을
   천명하였다.

첨 부 : 유엔가입문제에 관한 대한민국정부 각서 1부.   0065

유엔가입문제에 관한
대한민국정부 각서

대한민국 정부는 그간 유엔가입문제에 관한 입장과 특히 금년중 유엔가입을 실현코자 하는 결의를 누차 밝혀온 바 있음.

대한민국은 평화애호국가이며 유엔헌장상에 규정된 모든 의무를 수행할 의사와 능력이 있으므로, 유엔회원국으로서의 자격을 충분히 갖추고 있음. 세계 대부분의 국가와 외교관계를 맺고 있으며, 세계 제 12위의 교역국인 대한민국은, 유엔에 가입하여 유엔의 활동에 우리가 국제사회에서 차지하고 있는 위상에 부응하는 기여를 할 준비가 되어 있음.

유엔의 보편성원칙에 따라 유엔가입 요건을 갖추고 유엔가입을 희망하는 모든 주권국가는 유엔에 가입되어야 함. 탈냉전시대에 유엔이 보다 중요한 역할을 수행하게 됨에 따라 유엔의 보편성 원칙은 그 의미가 더욱 강화되고 있음. 화해와 협력의 새로운 정신으로 특징지워지는 전례없는 최근 국제정세의 변화속에서 이제는 한국의 유엔가입 문제가 해결되어야 함.

작년 제 45차 총회의 기조연설에서 잘 나타난 바와 같이 대한민국의 유엔가입이 더이상의 지체없이 실현되어야 한다는 것이 국제사회의 인식임.

대한민국은 유엔가입을 추진함에 있어, 조선민주주의인민공화국도 우리와 함께 또는 그들이 적절하다고 생각하는 시기에 유엔에 가입할 것을 진심으로 바라마지 않는바임. 대한민국은 북한의 유엔가입을 환영함을 재천명하는 바임.

뿐만 아니라, 대한민국은 남북한이 다함께 유엔에 가입하는 것이 통일이라는 궁극적 목표달성에 전혀 지장을 초래하지 않는다고 확신함. 남북한의 유엔가입은 남북한으로 하여금 유엔헌장상의 제규정과 원칙을 수락케 함으로써 한반도내의 강력한 신뢰구축 조치의 하나가 될 것임.

0066

유엔에 각각 별도로 가입했었던 동 .서독과 남 .북예멘의 통일은 이러한
우리의 견해가 타당하다는 점과 유엔가입이 분단을 고착화 또는 합법화하여
통일노력을 저해할 것이라는 주장이 부당하다는 것을 입증하고 있음.

국제사회가 한반도내에 남 .북한의 존재를 인정하여 왔음은 주지의 사실임.
현재 대한민국은 148개국과, 북한은 105개국과 각각 외교관계를 맺고 있으며
이중 90개국은 남북한과 동시수교관계를 맺고 있음. 또한 남북한은 많은 유엔
전문기구는 물론 대부분의 정부간 기구에 별도로 가입하고 있음. 따라서 이러한
국제정치 현실에서 남북한이 각각 유엔에 가입하는 것은 논리적으로 당연한 것임.

대한민국은 유엔가입이 한반도내의 평화와 안전을 증진할 뿐만 아니라
남북한간의 화해와 통일에 기여할 것이라는 신념에서 북한과 함께 유엔에 가입
하기 위하여 지난 한해동안 최선의 노력을 경주하여 왔으나 성과를 얻지 못하였음.

우리의 노력에도 불구하고, 북한은 실현불가능할 뿐만 아니라 유엔헌장의
규정과 유엔 및 그 전문기구의 제반 관행에도 배치되는 "단일의석 가입안"을
계속 고집하고 있음. 작년 유엔총회 기조연설에서 "단일의석 가입안"에 관하여
어느 회원국도 지지발언을 하지 않았던 사실만 보아도 "단일의석 가입안"이
유엔회원국들로부터 배척되고 있음을 잘 알수 있음.

대한민국정부는 금년중에 남북한이 다함께 유엔에 가입할 수 있기를 희망
하고 있음. 그러나 북한이 이러한 제안에 계속 반대하거나 또는 어떠한 이유로
유엔에 가입치 않을 것을 택한다면 대한민국은 주권을 행사하여 제 46차 유엔총회
개막이전 가입을 위한 필요한 조치를 취할 것임.

대한민국정부는 우리의 유엔가입 정당성에 대한 유엔회원국의 압도적
지지에 힘입어 향후 수개월내에 대한민국이 유엔에서 제자리를 차지할 수 있을
것이라고 확신하는 바임.

0067

MEMORANDUM OF THE GOVERNMENT OF THE REPUBLIC OF KOREA

5 April 1991

The Government of the Republic of Korea has made clear on previous occasions its position concerning membership of the Republic of Korea in the United Nations, particularly its determination to seek United Nations membership during the course of this year.

The Republic of Korea, as a peace-loving state willing and able to carry out all obligations set forth in the United Nations Charter, is fully qualified for membership in the United Nations. As a country which maintains almost universal diplomatic relations and as the world's twelfth largest trading nation, it is ready to make its due contribution to the work of the United Nations as a full Member and in a manner commensurate with its standing in the international community.

The principle of universality cherished by the United Nations requires the admission of all eligible sovereign states that wish to join the United Nations. This principle gains more relevance than ever as the United Nations assumes an increasingly vital role in the post-Cold War era. The unprecedented changes taking place in the international political environment, featuring a new spirit of reconciliation and cooperation, call for the resolution of Korea's membership question at long last.

As was eloquently manifested last year during the general debate of the 45th session of the General Assembly, it has become the sense of the international community that the admission of the Republic of Korea to United Nations membership should be realized without further delay.

/...

-1-

0068

In seeking United Nations membership, the Republic of Korea reiterates its earnest hope that the Democratic People's Republic of Korea(DPRK) will also join the United Nations, either together with the South, or at the time the North deems appropriate. The Republic of Korea restates its position that it would welcome DPRK's membership.

Furthermore, the Republic of Korea holds the view that the parallel membership of both Koreas in the United Nations is entirely without prejudice to the ultimate objective of Korea's reunification. Parallel membership should constitute a powerful confidence building measure insofar as it will represent a firm commitment of both Koreas to the provisions and principles of the United Nations Charter.

The unification of East and West Germany and of North and South Yemen, each of which had maintained separate membership in the United Nations, validates this view and disproves the contention that United Nations membership might serve to perpetuate or legitimize Korea's national division, thus hindering efforts for Korea's reunification.

It is a matter of fact that the international community has long recognized the existence of South and North Korea on the Korean Peninsula. In reality, the Republic of Korea and the DPRK maintain diplomatic relations with 146 and 105 countries respectively. Ninety of these countries maintain concurrent diplomatic relations with both. Each also has separate membership in most inter-governmental organizations, including specialized agencies of the United Nations. Thus, Korea's United Nations membership, separate or simultaneous, will be a logical corollary of the international political reality.

/...

-2-

In the sincere belief that United Nations membership will contribute to the process of Korean reconciliation and reunification, as well as enhance peace and security on the Korean Peninsula, the Republic of Korea has made every effort in good faith to join the United Nations together with the DPRK during the course of last year, but without success.

Despite these efforts, however, the DPRK has adhered to the 'single-seat membership' formula which is not only infeasible but runs counter to the provisions of the United Nations Charter and the practices followed by the United Nations and its specialized agenices. The lack of support from the United Nations Member States with respect to this formula during the general debate last year reflects their disapproval of the North Korean formula.

The Government of the Republic of Korea remains hopeful of realizing membership of both Koreas during the course of this year. However, if the DPRK continues to oppose this option and for any reason chooses not to join the United Nations, the Republic of Korea, exercising its sovereign right, will take the necessary step toward its membership before the opening of the 46th session of the General Assembly.

The Government of the Republic of Korea is convinced that, with the overwhelming support of the Member States of the United Nations for the legitimate cause of its membership, the Republic of Korea will be able to assume its rightful place in the United Nations in the months ahead.

- - - - -

-3-

국제기구국장 : ─ 외교장관보고후에 따라 다각설명 및
배포 ─ □3.

유엔加入에 관한 政府覺書 配布

1991. 4. 8.

外 務 部

유엔加入에 관한 우리 政府의 立場을 밝히는 覺書를
유엔 安保理文書로 配布토록 措置하였음을 報告드립니다.

1. 政府 覺書(1991. 4. 5字) 要旨

  o 우리는 유엔會員國 資格을 完全히 갖추고 있으며,
    유엔의 活動에 會員國으로서 積極 參與하길 希望함.

  o 우리는 北韓이 우리와 함께 유엔에 加入토록 지난해
    동안 努力하였으나 北韓은 實現 不可能한 單一議席
    加入案을 固執하고 있음.

  o 南北韓 유엔同時加入을 希望하는 우리의 立場에는
    변함이 없으나, 北韓이 이에 繼續 反對하거나,
    加入치 않기로 決定 하는 境遇, 우리는 今年中
    우리의 유엔加入 實現을 위한 必要한 措置를
    취할 것임.

  * 覺書文案은 美國등 核心友邦國과 事前 協議

0071

2. 유엔安保理 文書 配布

  o 上記 覺書는 今週初(4.8. 또는 4.9) 유엔安保理
     文書로서 유엔 全會員國 및 유엔傘下機構에 配布될
     豫定

3. 유엔加入 支持交涉,

  o 安保理 文書 配布 以前,
     - 유엔代表部에서 主要友邦國, 安保理 理事國 및
        主要 유엔會員國에 上記 覺書를 傳達하고 我國
        유엔加入 支持交涉 施行
     - 유엔駐在 中國, 蘇聯의 關係官을 接觸, 覺書
         內容을 說明하고 覺書 傳達
  o 유엔事務總長 및 安保理 非常任理事國 外務長官
     앞으로 同 覺書 內容을 中心으로 我國立場을
     說明하는 外務長官 書翰 發送 豫定
  o 駐韓外交使節앞 公翰添附, 同 覺書 配布 豫定

4. 弘報活動

  o 覺書 內容을 中心으로 유엔加入에 관한 우리立場을
     유엔 駐在 外國言論에 弘報하였으며, 國內言論을
     對象으로 報道資料 配布
  o 國會外務統一委소속 議員들에게 覺書 事前 配布
  o "外交問題 解說資料"를 作成하여 輿論指導層 6,000
     餘名을 對象으로 對國民 弘報 豫定

- 끝 -   0072

분류기호 문서번호	국연 2031- 125	협 조 문 용 지 (	)	결 재	담당	과장	국장
시행일자	1991. 4. 8.						
수 신	외교안보연구원장, 각실.국장	발 신	국제기구조약국장			(서명)	
제 목	유엔가입문제에 관한 각서 안보리 제출						

    1. 유엔가입문제에 관한 우리의 입장을 종합적으로 설명하고

금년중 유엔가입문제를 실현하고자 하는 의지를 밝히는 91.4.5.자

정부각서를 별첨 송부하오니 참고하시기 바랍니다.

    2. 동 각서는 금주초 (4.8. 또는 4.9) 유엔안보리 문서로 유엔

전회원국 및 유엔산하기구에 배포될 예정임을 알려드립니다.

    첨 부 : 각서 (국.영문) 각 1부.　　　　끝.

0073

유엔가입문제에 관한
대한민국정부 각서

대한민국 정부는 그간 유엔가입문제에 관한 입장과 특히 금년중 유엔
가입을 실현코자 하는 결의를 누차 밝혀온 바 있음.

대한민국은 유엔헌장상에 규정된 모든 의무를 수행할 의사와 능력이 있는
평화애호국가로서, 유엔회원국으로서의 자격을 충분히 갖추고 있음.   세계
대부분의 국가와 외교관계를 맺고 있으며, 세계 제 12위의 교역국인 대한민국은,
유엔에 가입하여 유엔의 활동에 우리가 국제사회에서 차지하고 있는 위상에 부응
하는 기여를 할 준비가 되어 있음.

유엔의 보편성원칙에 따라 가입 요건을 갖추고 유엔가입을 희망하는 모든
주권국가는 유엔에 가입되어야 함. 탈냉전시대에 유엔이 보다 중요한 역할을
수행하게 됨에 따라 유엔의 보편성 원칙은 그 의미가 더욱 강화되고 있음.
화해와 협력의 새로운 정신으로 특징지워지는 전례없는 최근 국제정세의 변화
속에서 이제는 한국의 유엔가입 문제가 해결되어야 함.

작년 제 45차 총회의 기조연설에서 잘 나타난 바와 같이 대한민국의 유엔
가입은 더이상의 지체없이 실현되어야 한다는 것이 국제사회의 인식이 되었음.

대한민국은 유엔가입을 추진함에 있어, 조선민주주의인민공화국도 함께
또는 그들이 적절하다고 생각하는 시기에 유엔에 가입할 것을 진심으로 바라마지
않는 바임. 대한민국은 북한의 유엔가입을 환영함을 재천명하는 바임.

뿐만 아니라, 대한민국은 남북한이 다함께 유엔에 가입하는 것이 통일이라는
궁극적 목표달성에 전혀 지장을 초래하지 않는다고 확신함. 남북한의 유엔가입은
남북한으로 하여금 유엔헌장상의 제규정과 원칙을 수락케 함으로써 강력한 신뢰
구축 조치의 하나가 될 것임.

0074

유엔에 각각 별도로 가입했었던 동.서독과 남.북예면의 통일은 이러한
우리의 견해가 타당하다는 점과 유엔가입이 분단을 고착화 또는 합법화하여
통일노력을 저해할 것이라는 주장이 부당하다는 것을 입증하고 있음.

국제사회가 한반도내 남.북한의 존재를 오랫동안 인정하여 왔음은 주지의
사실임. 현재 대한민국은 146개국과, 북한은 105개국과 각각 외교관계를 맺고
있으며 이중 90개국은 남북한과 동시수교관계를 맺고 있음. 또한 남북한은 많은
유엔전문기구는 물론 대부분의 정부간 기구에 별도로 가입하고 있음. 따라서
남북한이 각각 별도로 또는 동시에 유엔에 가입하는 것은 국제정치 현실의 당연한
논리적 귀결이 될 것임.

대한민국은 유엔가입이 한반도내의 평화와 안전을 증진할 뿐만 아니라
남북한간의 화해와 통일에 기여할 것이라는 신념에서 북한과 함께 유엔에 가입
하기 위하여 지난 한해동안 최선의 노력을 경주하여 왔으나 성과를 얻지 못하였음.

우리의 노력에도 불구하고, 북한은 실현불가능할 뿐만 아니라 유엔헌장의
규정과 유엔 및 그 전문기구의 제반 관행에도 배치되는 "단일의석 가입안"을
계속 고집하고 있음. 작년 유엔총회 기조연설에서 "단일의석 가입안"에 관하여
어느 회원국도 지지발언을 하지 않았던 사실만 보아도 "단일의석 가입안"이
유엔회원국들로부터 배척되고 있음을 잘 알수 있음.

대한민국정부는 금년중에 남북한이 다함께 유엔에 가입할 수 있기를 희망
하고 있음. 그러나 북한이 이러한 제안에 계속 반대하거나 또는 어떠한 이유로
유엔에 가입치 않을 것을 택한다면 대한민국은 주권을 행사하여 제 46차 유엔총회
개막이전 가입을 위한 필요한 조치를 취할 것임.

대한민국정부는 우리의 유엔가입 정당성에 대한 유엔회원국의 압도적
지지에 힘입어 향후 수개월내에 대한민국이 유엔에서 정당한 지위를 차지할 수
있을 것이라고 확신하는 바임.

0075

MEMORANDUM OF THE GOVERNMENT OF THE REPUBLIC OF KOREA

5 April 1991

The Government of the Republic of Korea has made clear on previous occasions its position concerning membership of the Republic of Korea in the United Nations, particularly its determination to seek United Nations membership during the course of this year.

The Republic of Korea, as a peace-loving state willing and able to carry out all obligations set forth in the United Nations Charter, is fully qualified for membership in the United Nations. As a country which maintains almost universal diplomatic relations and as the world's twelfth largest trading nation, it is ready to make its due contribution to the work of the United Nations as a full Member and in a manner commensurate with its standing in the international community.

The principle of universality cherished by the United Nations requires the admission of all eligible sovereign states that wish to join the United Nations. This principle gains more relevance than ever as the United Nations assumes an increasingly vital role in the post-Cold War era. The unprecedented changes taking place in the international political environment, featuring a new spirit of reconciliation and cooperation, call for the resolution of Korea's membership question at long last.

As was eloquently manifested last year during the general debate of the 45th session of the General Assembly, it has become the sense of the international community that the admission of the Republic of Korea to United Nations membership should be realized without further delay.

/...

-1-

0076

In seeking United Nations membership, the Republic of Korea reiterates its earnest hope that the Democratic People's Republic of Korea(DPRK) will also join the United Nations, either together with the South, or at the time the North deems appropriate. The Republic of Korea restates its position that it would welcome DPRK's membership.

Furthermore, the Republic of Korea holds the view that the parallel membership of both Koreas in the United Nations is entirely without prejudice to the ultimate objective of Korea's reunification. Parallel membership should constitute a powerful confidence building measure insofar as it will represent a firm commitment of both Koreas to the provisions and principles of the United Nations Charter.

The unification of East and West Germany and of North and South Yemen, each of which had maintained separate membership in the United Nations, validates this view and disproves the contention that United Nations membership might serve to perpetuate or legitimize Korea's national division, thus hindering efforts for Korea's reunification.

It is a matter of fact that the international community has long recognized the existence of South and North Korea on the Korean Peninsula. In reality, the Republic of Korea and the DPRK maintain diplomatic relations with 146 and 105 countries respectively. Ninety of these countries maintain concurrent diplomatic relations with both. Each also has separate membership in most inter-governmental organizations, including specialized agencies of the United Nations. Thus, Korea's United Nations membership, separate or simultaneous, will be a logical corollary of the international political reality.

/...

-2-

0077

In the sincere belief that United Nations membership will contribute to the process of Korean reconciliation and reunification, as well as enhance peace and security on the Korean Peninsula, the Republic of Korea has made every effort in good faith to join the United Nations together with the DPRK during the course of last year, but without success.

Despite these efforts, however, the DPRK has adhered to the 'single-seat membership' formula which is not only infeasible but runs counter to the provisions of the United Nations Charter and the practices followed by the United Nations and its specialized agenices. The lack of support from the United Nations Member States with respect to this formula during the general debate last year reflects their disapproval of the North Korean formula.

The Government of the Republic of Korea remains hopeful of realizing membership of both Koreas during the course of this year. However, if the DPRK continues to oppose this option and for any reason chooses not to join the United Nations, the Republic of Korea, exercising its sovereign right, will take the necessary step toward its membership before the opening of the 46th session of the General Assembly.

The Government of the Republic of Korea is convinced that, with the overwhelming support of the Member States of the United Nations for the legitimate cause of its membership, the Republic of Korea will be able to assume its rightful place in the United Nations in the months ahead.

- - - - -

-3-

분류기호 문서번호	국연 2031-	기 안 용 지 (전화 :　　　　　)	시 행 상 특별취급	
보존기간	영구·준영구. 10. 5. 3. 1.	장 　　　 관		
수 신 처 보존기간				
시행일자	1991. 4. 8.			

보 조 기 관	국 장	전 결	협 조 기 관		문 서 통 제	1991. 4. 08
	과 장					
기안책임자	송 영 환				발 송 인	

경 유 수 신 참 조	수신처 참조	발 신 명 의	
제 목	유연가입에 관한 정부 각서		

유연가입에 관한 우리정부의 입장과 금년중 유연가입을 실현

코자 하는 의지를 밝히는 메모랜덤이 금주초 (4.8. 또는 4.9) 안보리

문서로 배포될 예정인 바, 동 메모랜덤을 별첨 송부하니 업무에 참고

하시기 바랍니다.

　

　첨 부 : 메모랜덤 1부.　　　끝.

　수신처 : 국토통일원장관, 국가안전기획부장, 공보처장

0073

1505-25(2-1) 일(1)갑
85. 9. 9. 승인　　"내가아낀 종이 한장 늘어나는 나라살림"
190mm×268mm　인쇄용지 2 급　60g/㎡
가 40-41　1989. 6. 8

MEMORANDUM OF THE GOVERNMENT OF THE REPUBLIC OF KOREA

5 April 1991

The Government of the Republic of Korea has made clear on previous occasions its position concerning membership of the Republic of Korea in the United Nations, particularly its determination to seek United Nations membership during the course of this year.

The Republic of Korea, as a peace-loving state willing and able to carry out all obligations set forth in the United Nations Charter, is fully qualified for membership in the United Nations. As a country which maintains almost universal diplomatic relations and as the world's twelfth largest trading nation, it is ready to make its due contribution to the work of the United Nations as a full Member and in a manner commensurate with its standing in the international community.

The principle of universality cherished by the United Nations requires the admission of all eligible sovereign states that wish to join the United Nations. This principle gains more relevance than ever as the United Nations assumes an increasingly vital role in the post-Cold War era. The unprecedented changes taking place in the international political environment, featuring a new spirit of reconciliation and cooperation, call for the resolution of Korea's membership question at long last.

As was eloquently manifested last year during the general debate of the 45th session of the General Assembly, it has become the sense of the international community that the admission of the Republic of Korea to United Nations membership should be realized without further delay.

/...

-1-

0080

In seeking United Nations membership, the Republic of Korea reiterates its earnest hope that the Democratic People's Republic of Korea(DPRK) will also join the United Nations, either together with the South, or at the time the North deems appropriate. The Republic of Korea restates its position that it would welcome DPRK's membership.

Furthermore, the Republic of Korea holds the view that the parallel membership of both Koreas in the United Nations is entirely without prejudice to the ultimate objective of Korea's reunification. Parallel membership should constitute a powerful confidence building measure insofar as it will represent a firm commitment of both Koreas to the provisions and principles of the United Nations Charter.

The unification of East and West Germany and of North and South Yemen, each of which had maintained separate membership in the United Nations, validates this view and disproves the contention that United Nations membership might serve to perpetuate or legitimize Korea's national division, thus hindering efforts for Korea's reunification.

It is a matter of fact that the international community has long recognized the existence of South and North Korea on the Korean Peninsula. In reality, the Republic of Korea and the DPRK maintain diplomatic relations with 146 and 105 countries respectively. Ninety of these countries maintain concurrent diplomatic relations with both. Each also has separate membership in most inter-governmental organizations, including specialized agencies of the United Nations. Thus, Korea's United Nations membership, separate or simultaneous, will be a logical corollary of the international political reality.

/...

-2-

0081

In the sincere belief that United Nations membership will contribute to the process of Korean reconciliation and reunification, as well as enhance peace and security on the Korean Peninsula, the Republic of Korea has made every effort in good faith to join the United Nations together with the DPRK during the course of last year, but without success.

Despite these efforts, however, the DPRK has adhered to the 'single-seat membership' formula which is not only infeasible but runs counter to the provisions of the United Nations Charter and the practices followed by the United Nations and its specialized agenices. The lack of support from the United Nations Member States with respect to this formula during the general debate last year reflects their disapproval of the North Korean formula.

The Government of the Republic of Korea remains hopeful of realizing membership of both Koreas during the course of this year. However, if the DPRK continues to oppose this option and for any reason chooses not to join the United Nations, the Republic of Korea, exercising its sovereign right, will take the necessary step toward its membership before the opening of the 46th session of the General Assembly.

The Government of the Republic of Korea is convinced that, with the overwhelming support of the Member States of the United Nations for the legitimate cause of its membership, the Republic of Korea will be able to assume its rightful place in the United Nations in the months ahead.

- - - - -

0082

외 무 부

종 별 : 지 급

번 호 : UNW-0834

수 신 : 장 관(국연)

발 신 : 주 유엔 대사

제 목 : 안보리문서 배포

일 시 : 91 0408 1840

대: WUN-0795

대호 각서가 금 4.8.(월) 안보리 문서로 배포된바, 동 각서 영어, 불어, 서반어, 중국어, 소련어, 아랍어본을 별첨 FAX 송부함.

첨부:상기 문서 각1부:UNW(F)-159

끝

(대사 노창희-국장)

국기국

PAGE 1

UNW(FI)-159   104.번 1840

(국연)

총 25대   S

UNITED NATIONS

Security Council

Distr.
GENERAL

S/22455
5 April 1991

ORIGINAL: ENGLISH

NOTE BY THE PRESIDENT OF THE SECURITY COUNCIL

The attached letter dated 5 April 1991 from the Permanent Observer of the Republic of Korea to the United Nations was addressed to the President of the Security Council. In accordance with the request therein contained, the letter is being circulated as a document of the Security Council.

91-11147 2247h (E)

/...

#UNW-0834
청부몰

25-1

0084

Annex

Letter dated 5 April 1991 from the Permanent Observer of the
Republic of Korea to the United Nations addressed to the
President of the Security Council

Upon instructions from my Government, I have the honour to transmit to you a memorandum of the Government of the Republic of Korea concerning its membership in the United Nations.

I should be grateful if you would have the text of this letter and the enclosed memorandum circulated as a document of the Security Council.

(Signed) Chang Hee ROE
Ambassador

/...

25-2

0085

Enclosure

Memorandum of the Government of the Republic of Korea

    The Government of the Republic of Korea has made clear on previous occasions its position concerning membership of the Republic of Korea in the United Nations, particularly its determination to seek United Nations membership during the course of this year.

    The Republic of Korea, as a peace-loving State willing and able to carry out all obligations set forth in the United Nations Charter, is fully qualified for membership in the United Nations. As a country which maintains almost universal diplomatic relations and as the world's twelfth largest trading nation, it is ready to make its due contribution to the work of the United Nations as a full member and in a manner commensurate with its standing in the international community.

    The principle of universality cherished by the United Nations requires the admission of all eligible sovereign States that wish to join the United Nations. This principle gains more relevance than ever as the United Nations assumes an increasingly vital role in the post-cold war era. The unprecedented changes taking place in the international political environment, featuring a new spirit of reconciliation and cooperation, call for the resolution of Korea's membership question at long last.

    As was eloquently manifested last year during the general debate of the forty-fifth session of the General Assembly, it has become the sense of the international community that the admission of the Republic of Korea to United Nations membership should be realized without further delay.

    In seeking United Nations membership, the Republic of Korea reiterates its earnest hope that the Democratic People's Republic of Korea (DPRK) will also join the United Nations, either together with the South, or at the time the North deems appropriate. The Republic of Korea restates its position that it would welcome DPRK's membership.

    Furthermore, the Republic of Korea holds the view that the parallel membership of both Koreas in the United Nations is entirely without prejudice to the ultimate objective of Korea's reunification. Parallel membership should constitute a powerful confidence-building measure in so far as it will represent a firm commitment of both Koreas to the provisions and principles of the United Nations Charter.

    The unification of East and West Germany and of North and South Yemen, each of which had maintained separate membership in the United Nations, validates this view and disproves the contention that United Nations membership might serve to perpetuate or legitimize Korea's national division, thus hindering efforts for Korea's reunification.

/...

25-3

0086

S/22455
English
Page 4

It is a matter of fact that the international community has long recognized the existence of South and North Korea on the Korean peninsula. In reality, the Republic of Korea and the DPRK maintain diplomatic relations with 148 and 105 countries respectively. Ninety of these countries maintain concurrent diplomatic relations with both. Each also has separate membership in most intergovernmental organizations, including specialized agencies of the United Nations. Thus, Korea's United Nations membership, separate or simultaneous, will be a logical corollary of the international political reality.

In the sincere belief that United Nations membership will contribute to the process of Korean reconciliation and reunification, as well as enhance peace and security on the Korean peninsula, the Republic of Korea has made every effort in good faith to join the United Nations together with the DPRK during the course of last year, but without success.

Despite these efforts, however, the DPRK has adhered to the "single-seat membership" formula which is not only unworkable, but runs counter to the provisions of the United Nations Charter and the practices followed by the United Nations and its specialized agencies. The lack of support from the United Nations Member States with respect to this formula during the general debate last year reflects their disapproval of the North Korean formula.

The Government of the Republic of Korea remains hopeful of realizing the membership of both Koreas during the course of this year. However, if the DPRK continues to oppose this option and for any reason chooses not to join the United Nations, the Republic of Korea, exercising its sovereign right, will take the necessary step towards its membership before the opening of the forty-sixth session of the General Assembly.

The Government of the Republic of Korea is convinced that, with the overwhelming support of the Member States of the United Nations for the legitimate cause of its membership, the Republic of Korea will be able to assume its rightful place in the United Nations in the months ahead.

0087

NATIONS UNIES

Conseil de sécurité

Distr.
GENERALE

S/22455
5 avril 1991
FRANCAIS
ORIGINAL : ANGLAIS

NOTE DU PRESIDENT DU CONSEIL DE SECURITE

La lettre jointe, datée du 5 avril 1991, a été adressée au Président du
Conseil de sécurité par l'Observateur permanent de la République de Corée auprès de
l'Organisation des Nations Unies. Conformément à la demande qui y est formulée,
elle est distribuée en tant que document du Conseil de sécurité.

91-11148   4886V   (F)

/...

0088

25-5

S/22455
Français
Page 2

ANNEXE

Lettre datée du 5 avril 1991, adressée au Président du Conseil de sécurité par l'Observateur permanent de la République de Corée auprès de l'Organisation des Nations Unies

D'ordre de mon gouvernement, j'ai l'honneur de vous faire tenir ci-joint un mémorandum du Gouvernement de la République de Corée concernant son admission à l'Organisation des Nations Unies.

Je vous serais très obligé de bien vouloir faire distribuer le texte de la présente lettre et du mémorandum joint comme document du Conseil de sécurité.

L'Ambassadeur

(Signé) Chang Hee ROE

0089

/...

PIECE JOINTE

Mémorandum du Gouvernement de la République de Corée

Le Gouvernement de la République de Corée a déjà, à plusieurs occasions, précisé sa position concernant l'admission de la République de Corée à l'Organisation des Nations Unies, et en particulier sa volonté de demander cette admission cette année.

La République de Corée, Etat épris de paix, désireux et capable d'assumer toutes les obligations énoncées dans la Charte des Nations Unies, a pleinement qualité pour être admise à l'ONU. Elle entretient des relations diplomatiques avec la quasi universalité des pays et occupe le douzième rang dans le commerce mondial, et elle est disposée à apporter à l'action de l'ONU la contribution qu'on peut attendre d'elle en tant que membre à part entière, et à la mesure de sa position dans la communauté internationale.

Le principe d'universalité auquel souscrit l'Organisation a pour corollaire l'obligation d'y admettre tous les Etats souverains qui souhaitent y entrer et réunissent les conditions voulues. Ce principe est plus valable que jamais au moment où l'Organisation assume un rôle de plus en plus décisif au lendemain de la guerre froide. Les changements inouïs qui se produisent dans le climat politique international, et qui marquent l'avènement d'un nouvel esprit de réconciliation et de coopération, invitent à régler enfin la question de l'admission de la Corée.

Comme l'a éloquemment montré, l'an dernier, le débat général de la quarante-cinquième session de l'Assemblée générale, la communauté internationale a maintenant le sentiment que l'entrée de la République de Corée à l'ONU ne peut plus être différée.

En demandant son admission à l'Organisation des Nations Unies, la République de Corée réitère son espoir sincère que la République populaire démocratique de Corée (RPDC) entrera également à l'ONU, soit au même moment que le Sud, soit quand le Nord le jugera opportun. La République de Corée réaffirme sa position, à savoir qu'elle saluerait l'admission de la RPDC.

En outre, la République de Corée estime que l'admission parallèle des deux Corée à l'ONU ne préjuge en rien la question de l'objectif ultime qu'est la réunification du pays. La présence simultanée des deux Corée à l'ONU constituerait une puissante mesure de renforcement de la confiance, car elle témoignerait de la ferme volonté des deux Corée de se conformer aux dispositions et aux principes de la Charte des Nations Unies.

L'unification de l'Allemagne de l'Est et de l'Ouest et du Yémen du Nord et du Sud, qui précédemment occupaient chacun un siège à l'ONU, conforte cette façon de voir et réfute l'idée que l'admission à l'Organisation des Nations Unies pourrait avoir pour effet de perpétuer ou de légitimer la division de la nation coréenne et risquerait par-là d'entraver les efforts de réunification.

/...

25-7

0090

S/22455
Français
Page 4

La communauté internationale a, en vérité, admis depuis longtemps l'existence
dans la péninsule coréenne d'une Corée du Sud et d'une Corée du Nord. Le fait est
que la République de Corée et la RPDC entretiennent respectivement des relations
diplomatiques avec 148 et 105 pays. Quatre-vingt-dix de ces pays entretiennent
simultanément des relations diplomatiques avec l'une et l'autre. Chacune des deux
a été admise séparément dans la plupart des organisations intergouvernementales,
y compris certaines institutions spécialisées de l'ONU. Ainsi l'admission séparée
ou simultanée des deux Corée à l'Organisation des Nations Unies serait le
corollaire logique de la situation politique internationale réelle.

Sincèrement convaincue que l'admission de la République de Corée à
l'Organisation des Nations Unies contribuerait à la réconciliation en Corée et à la
réunification du pays et servirait la cause de la paix et de la sécurité dans la
péninsule, la République de Corée, en toute bonne foi, n'a épargné aucun effort
pour entrer à l'ONU, avec la RPDC, l'an dernier, mais sans succès.

En dépit de ces efforts, pourtant, la RPDC s'en tient à la formule "du siège
unique" qui non seulement ne peut fonctionner, mais est contraire aux dispositions
de la Charte des Nations Unies et à la pratique suivie par l'ONU et par ses
institutions spécialisées. Le fait que les Etats Membres de l'ONU n'ont pas repris
cette formule à leur compte, pendant le débat général, l'an dernier, porte
témoignage de leur désapprobation de la formule nord-coréenne.

Le Gouvernement de la République de Corée continue à espérer que les deux
Corée seront admises à l'ONU cette année. Cependant, si la RPDC continue à
s'opposer à cette solution, et, pour une raison quelconque, décide de ne pas entrer
à l'ONU, la République de Corée, exerçant les droits afférents à sa souveraineté,
fera ce qu'il faudra pour devenir un Etat Membre avant l'ouverture de la
quarante-sixième session de l'Assemblée générale.

Le Gouvernement de la République de Corée est convaincu que, forte du soutien
massif des Etats Membres pour le principe légitime de son admission, la République
de Corée pourra dans les mois qui viennent prendre la place qui lui revient au sein
des Nations Unies.

0091

NACIONES UNIDAS

Consejo de Seguridad

Distr.
GENERAL

S/22455
5 de abril de 1991
ESPAÑOL
ORIGINAL: INGLES

NOTA DEL PRESIDENTE DEL CONSEJO DE SEGURIDAD

La carta de fecha 5 de abril de 1991 que figura en el anexo fue dirigida al Presidente del Consejo de Seguridad por el Observador Permanente de la República de Corea ante las Naciones Unidas. Conforme a lo solicitado, se procede a su distribución como documento del Consejo de Seguridad.

91-11150   2088a

/...

25-9

0092

S/22455
Español
Página 2

ANEXO

Carta de fecha 5 de abril de 1991 dirigida al Presidente del Consejo
de Seguridad por el Observador Permanente de la República de Corea
ante las Naciones Unidas

Siguiendo instrucciones de mi Gobierno, tengo el honor de transmitirle un
memorando del Gobierno de la República de Corea relativo a su admisión en las
Naciones Unidas.

Le agradecería que tuviera a bien hacer distribuir el texto de la presente
carta y el memorando adjunto como documento del Consejo de Seguridad.

(Firmado)   Chang Hee ROE
Embajador

0093
/...

25-10

APENDICE

Memorando del Gobierno de la República de Corea

El Gobierno de la República de Corea ha expresado claramente en ocasiones anteriores su posición con respecto a la admisión en las Naciones Unidas, y, en particular, su determinación de solicitarla en el curso del presente año.

La República de Corea, que es un Estado pacífico, deseoso de cumplir todas las obligaciones enunciadas en la Carta de las Naciones Unidas y capaz de hacerlo, reúne todas las condiciones necesarias para ser Miembro de las Naciones Unidas. Tratándose de un país que mantiene relaciones diplomáticas casi universales y ocupa el duodécimo lugar mundial en cuanto a volumen comercial, la República de Corea está dispuesta a contribuir debidamente a la labor de las Naciones Unidas como Miembro pleno y de forma consecuente con su posición en la comunidad internacional.

El principio de universalidad consagrado por las Naciones Unidas impone la admisión de todos los Estados soberanos que reúnan las condiciones necesarias y deseen pertenecer a la Organización. Este principio cobra más importancia que nunca en momentos en que las Naciones Unidas asumen un papel cada vez más vital en la era posterior a la guerra fría. Los cambios sin precedentes que tienen lugar en las circunstancias políticas internacionales, y que revelan un nuevo espíritu de reconciliación y de cooperación, exigen que se decida por fin la cuestión del ingreso de Corea.

Como se manifestó elocuentemente el año pasado durante el debate general del cuadragésimo quinto período de sesiones de la Asamblea, la comunidad internacional ha tomado conciencia de que la República de Corea debe ser admitida sin más demora en las Naciones Unidas.

Al aspirar a la condición de Miembro de las Naciones Unidas, la República de Corea reitera su ferviente esperanza de que la República Popular Democrática de Corea (RPDC) también ingrese a las Naciones Unidas, ya bien junto con el Sur, o en el momento en que el Norte lo estime apropiado. La República de Corea declara una vez más su posición de que acogerá con agrado la admisión de la RPDC.

Además, en opinión de la República de Corea, la presencia simultánea de las dos Coreas en las Naciones Unidas no menoscaba en modo alguno el objetivo último de su reunificación. La presencia simultánea debería constituir una poderosa medida de fomento de la confianza por cuanto representará la firme adhesión de los dos Estados a las disposiciones y los principios de la Carta de las Naciones Unidas.

La unificación de Alemania Oriental y Alemania Occidental y del Yemen del Norte y del Sur, cada uno de los cuales fue Miembro de las Naciones Unidas por separado, confiere validez a esta opinión y refuta el argumento de que la admisión en las Naciones Unidas podría servir para perpetuar o legitimar la división nacional de Corea, y obstaculizar así los esfuerzos en pro de su reunificación.

/...

25-11

0094

S/22455
Español
Página 4

La realidad es que la comunidad internacional reconoció hace tiempo la
existencia de Corea del Sur y Corea del Norte en la misma península. De hecho, la
República de Corea y la RPDC mantienen relaciones diplomáticas con 148 y 105 países
respectivamente, y 90 de esos países mantienen relaciones diplomáticas con ambas.
Asimismo, cada una de ellas es, por separado, miembro de la mayor parte de las
organizaciones interguvernamentales, incluidos los organismos especializados de las
Naciones Unidas. Por ende, la admisión de Corea en las Naciones Unidas, ya sea por
separado o de forma simultánea, será el corolario lógico de la realidad política
internacional.

La República de Corea está sinceramente convencida de que el ingreso en las
Naciones Unidas contribuirá al proceso de reconciliación y reunificación de Corea y
a la vez promoverá la paz y la seguridad en la península de Corea. En
consecuencia, durante el pasado año, hizo de buena fe cuanto estuvo a su alcance
por incorporarse a las Naciones Unidas junto con la RPDC. Lamentablemente sus
gestiones resultaron infructuosas.

En cambio, la RPDC es partidaria del ingreso de una sola representación,
fórmula que no sólo es impracticable, sino que además atenta contra las
disposiciones de la Carta de las Naciones Unidas y contra las prácticas de la
Organización y sus organismos especializados. La falta de apoyo de los Estados
Miembros de las Naciones Unidas durante el debate general celebrado el año pasado
demuestra que no aprueban la fórmula de Corea del Norte.

El Gobierno de la República de Corea mantiene la esperanza de que las dos
Coreas sean admitidas el presente año. Ahora bien, si la RPDC se sigue oponiendo a
esta opción, y por cualquier motivo decide no incorporarse a las Naciones Unidas,
la República de Corea, en ejercicio de su derecho soberano, hará las gestiones
necesarias para ser admitida antes de la inauguración del cuadragésimo sexto
período de sesiones de la Asamblea General.

El Gobierno de la República de Corea está persuadido de que, al contar con el
abrumador apoyo de los Estados Miembros de las Naciones Unidas a la legítima causa
de su admisión, en los meses venideros la República de Corea podrá ocupar el lugar
que legítimamente le corresponde en las Naciones Unidas.

0095

ОРГАНИЗАЦИЯ
ОБЪЕДИНЕННЫХ НАЦИЙ

S

 Совет Безопасности

Distr.
GENERAL

S/22455
5 April 1991
RUSSIAN
ORIGINAL: ENGLISH

ЗАПИСКА ПРЕДСЕДАТЕЛЯ СОВЕТА БЕЗОПАСНОСТИ

На имя Председателя Совета Безопасности поступило прилагаемое письмо Постоянного наблюдателя Республики Кореи при Организации Объединенных Наций от 5 апреля 1991 года. В соответствии с содержащейся в нем просьбой настоящее письмо распространяется в качестве документа Совета Безопасности.

S/22455
Russian
Page 2

Приложение

<u>Письмо Постоянного наблюдателя Республики Кореи при Организации
Объединенных Наций от 5 апреля 1991 года на имя Председателя
Совета Безопасности</u>

По поручению моего правительства имею честь препроводить Вам меморандум
правительства Республики Кореи, касающийся ее вступления в члены Организации
Объединенных Наций.

Буду признателен Вам за распространение настоящего письма и прилагаемого к
нему меморандума в качестве документа Совета Безопасности.

Чанг Хи РО
Посол

/...

25-14

0097

Добавление

Меморандум правительства Республики Кореи

Правительство Республики Кореи ранее недвусмысленно заявляло о своей позиции относительно членства Республики Кореи в Организации Объединенных Наций, особенно о своей решимости добиваться вступления в члены Организации Объединенных Наций в течение этого года.

Республика Корея, будучи миролюбивым государством, которое стремится и в состоянии выполнять все обязательства, содержащиеся в Уставе Организации Объединенных Наций, отвечает всем требованиям, необходимым для вступления в члены Организации Объединенных Наций. Являясь страной, которая поддерживает дипломатические отношения почти со всеми странами мира, и государством, занимающим двенадцатое место в мире в ряду крупнейших торговых держав, Республика Корея готова внести свой должный вклад в деятельность Организации Объединенных Наций в качестве полноправного члена и в соответствии со своим положением в международном сообществе.

Принцип универсальности, на который опирается Организация Объединенных Наций, предполагает как необходимое условие вступление в члены Организации Объединенных Наций всех суверенных государств, которые выражают такое желание и имеют на это право. Этот принцип как никогда приобретает особую актуальность, поскольку Организация Объединенных Наций играет все более важную роль в эпоху после окончания "холодной войны". Беспрецедентные изменения, происходящие на международной политической арене, отражающие новый дух примирения и сотрудничества, обусловливают необходимость окончательного решения вопроса о вступлении Кореи в Организацию Объединенных Наций.

Как справедливо отмечалось в прошлом году в ходе общих прений на сорок пятой сессии Генеральной Ассамблеи, международное сообщество осознало, что Республика Корея должна без дальнейших промедлений вступить в члены Организации Объединенных Наций.

Стремясь стать членом Организации Объединенных Наций, Республика Корея вновь выражает искреннюю надежду на то, что Корейская Народно-Демократическая Республика (КНДР) также вступит в Организацию Объединенных Наций либо одновременно с Южной Кореей, либо в тот момент, когда Северная Корея сочтет это необходимым. Республика Корея подтверждает свою позицию, заключающуюся в том, что она будет приветствовать вступление КНДР в члены Организации Объединенных Наций.

Кроме того, Республика Корея придерживается той точки зрения, что параллельное членство двух корейских государств в Организации Объединенных Наций никоим образом не наносит ущерба конечной цели объединения Кореи. Параллельное членство должно представлять собой действенную меру укрепления доверия, поскольку оно будет означать твердую приверженность двух корейских государств положениям и принципам Устава Организации Объединенных Наций.

/...

25-15

0098

S/22455
Russian
Page 4

Объединение Восточной и Западной Германии, а также Северного и Южного Йемена в условиях, когда каждое государство сохраняло раздельное членство в Организации Объединенных Наций, подтверждает эту точку зрения и лишает смысла утверждение о том, что членство в Организации Объединенных Наций может увековечить или узаконить разделение корейской нации, препятствуя тем самым усилиям, направленным на объединение Кореи.

Реальность такова, что международное сообщество в течение долгого времени признавало существование Южной и Северной Кореи на Корейском полуострове. Действительно, Корейская Республика и КНДР поддерживают дипломатические отношения со 148 и 105 странами, соответственно. Из этого числа 90 стран поддерживают одновременно дипломатические отношения с обоими корейскими государствами. Каждое корейское государство также отдельно представлено в большинстве межправительственных организаций, включая специализированные учреждения Организации Объединенных Наций. Таким образом, членство Кореи в Организации Объединенных Наций - раздельное или параллельное - станет логическим следствием международной политической реальности.

Будучи искренне убеждена в том, что членство в Организации Объединенных Наций будет содействовать процессу примирения в Корее и ее объединению, а также укреплению мира и безопасности на Корейском полуострове, Республика Корея в духе доброй воли предпринимала все возможные усилия с целью вступления в члены Организации Объединенных Наций одновременно с КНДР в прошлом году, однако эти усилия не увенчались успехом.

Однако, несмотря на эти усилия, КНДР придерживается формулы "единая делегация - одно место", которая не только является непригодной, но и противоречит положениям Устава Организации Объединенных Наций и практике, применяемой Организацией Объединенных Наций и ее специализированными учреждениями. Отсутствие поддержки этой формулы со стороны государств - членов Организации Объединенных Наций в ходе общих прений в прошлом году свидетельствует об их несогласии с формулой Северной Кореи.

Правительство Республики Корея по-прежнему надеется на вступление двух корейских государств в члены Организации Объединенных Наций в течение этого года. Однако, если КНДР будет и впредь выступать против такого возможного варианта и по каким бы то ни было причинам предпочтет не вступать в члены Организации Объединенных Наций, Республика Корея в порядке осуществления своего суверенного права предпримет необходимые шаги, направленные на ее вступление в Организацию Объединенных Наций до открытия сорок шестой сессии Генеральной Ассамблеи.

Правительство Республики Корея убеждено в том, что при подавляющей поддержке ее законного стремления вступить в члены Организации Объединенных Наций со стороны государств - членов Организации Республика Корея сможет занять принадлежащее ей по праву место в Организации Объединенных Наций в течение предстоящих месяцев.

25-16

0099

联合国

 安全理事会

Distr.
GENERAL

S/22455
5 April 1991
CHINESE
ORIGINAL: ENGLISH

安全理事会主席的说明

　　所附为1991年4月5日大韩民国常驻联合国观察员给联合国安全理事会主席的信。兹依照信内要求，将此信作为安全理事会的文件散发。

91-11146

25-17

0100

S/22455
Chinese
Page 2

附 件

1991年4月5日
大韩民国常驻联合国观察员
给安全理事会主席的信

奉我国政府指示,谨转递大韩民国政府关于其联合国会员籍的备忘录。

谨请将本信全文及所附备忘录作为安全理事会文件散发为荷。

大使

卢昌熹(签名)

0101

附　文

大韩民国政府备忘录

　　大韩民国政府在过去已在许多场合表明其对于大韩民国在联合国会籍所持的立场，特别是关于大韩民国在本年内争取联合国会员籍的决心。

　　大韩民国，作为一个愿意且能够履行《联合国宪章》规定的一切义务的爱好和平的国家，完全有资格成为联合国的会员国。作为与全世界几乎所有的国家都维持外交关系的，世界第十二大贸易国，大韩民国已准备好愿以联合国充分会员身份与在国际社会所处地位相衬的方式对联合国的工作作出应有的贡献。

　　联合国所重视的普遍性原则要求允许希望加入联合国的一切有资格的主权国家都加入联合国。随着联合国在冷战后的时代承担日益重要的角色，这个普遍性原则比以往任何时候更显得重要。国际政治环境里发生的以和解与合作的新精神为特点的史无前例的变化，终于要求解决韩国会员籍的问题。

　　正如去年大会第四十五届会议一般性辩论中令人信服地显示的，整个国际社会都感觉到，不应该再拖延实现大韩民国加入联合国了。

　　大韩民国在争取加入为联合国会员国时，重申其热切盼望朝鲜民主主义人民共和国（北朝鲜）也与南韩同时，或在北朝鲜认为适当的时候，加入联合国。大韩民国重申它欢迎北朝鲜加入联合国的立场。

　　此外，大韩民国始终认为两韩在联合国内的平行会员籍是完全不影响韩国统一的最终目标的。平行会员籍，只要它代表两韩对《联合国宪章》的规定和原则的坚定承诺，就应该是一项有力的建立信心的措施。

　　东西德国和南北也门两国在联合国中都曾保持过分开的会员籍。这两国的统一支持了此一意见而否定了联合国会员籍可能会延续或使韩国的民族分裂合法化从而阻碍了韩国统一努力的说法。

25-19

S/22455
Chinese
Page 4

   实际上国际社会早已承认了韩国半岛上南北韩的存在。事实是,大韩民国与北朝鲜分别与148和105个国家保持外交关系。九十个国家与两边都保持并行的外交关系。南北双方也分别在大多数政府间组织,包括联合国专门机构享有会员籍。因此,韩国的联合国会员籍,不论分开的或并存的,都将是国际政治现实的逻辑必然结果。

   去年,大韩民国由于真心相信联合国会员籍会有助于韩国和解与统一的进程,以及增进韩国半岛的和平与安全,所以诚意地作出一切努力,争取同北朝鲜一道加入联合国,但未成功。

   然而,尽管这样的努力,北朝鲜还是坚守"单一会员国席位"的方式,这不仅是行不通,并且与《联合国宪章》的规定和联合国及其专门机构采取的作法背道而驰。去年一般辩论期间,联合国会员国对这一方式缺乏支持反映了它们对这一北朝鲜方式的不赞同。

   大韩民国政府仍然希望今年内韩国两方的会员籍能够实现。然而,如果北朝鲜继续反对这一备选办法,并且不论用任何理由而选择不加入联合国,则大韩民国将行使其主权权利,在大会第四十六届会议开幕前采取为取得会员籍的必要步骤。

   大韩民国政府深信,在联合国会员国对其争取会员籍的正当事业的绝大多数支持下,几个月后大韩民国将能够取得其在联合国的正当地位。

- - - - -

0103

الأمم المتحدة

Distr.
GENERAL

S/22455
5 April 1991
ARABIC
ORIGINAL : ENGLISH

مجلس الأمن

مذكرة من رئيس مجلس الامن

وجه المراقب الدائم عن جمهورية كوريا لدى الامم المتحدة إلى رئيس مجلس الامن
الرسالة المرفقة المؤرخة ٥ نيسان/ابريل ١٩٩١ . ووفقا للطلب الوارد فيها تعمم هـذه
الرسالة بوصفها وثيقة من وثائق مجلس الامن .

../..

(٩١)ق.٠٧٧ 91-11145

25 - 21

0104

-۲-

مرفق

<u>رسالـــة مؤرخـــة فـــي ٥ نيسان/ابريـــل ١٩٩١</u>
<u>موجهة إلى رئيـــس مجلـــس الامن مـــن المراقب</u>
<u>الدائم عن جمهوريـــة كوريا لدى الامم المتحدة</u>

بنـــاءً على تعليمات من حكومتي اتشرف بـان احيل إليكم طيه مذكرة من حكومـــة
جمهورية كوريا بشان انضمامها الى عضوية الامم المتحدة .

واغدو ممتنًا لو تفظلتم بتعميم نص هذه الرسالة والمذكرة المرفقة بهـــا ،
بوصفهما وثيقة من وثائق مجلس الامن .

(توقيع) شائغ هي رو
السفير

../..

(٩١)ف.٥٧٧

25-22

0105

S/22455
Arabic
Page 3   -٢-

ضميمة

مذكرة من حكومة جمهورية كوريا

أوضحت حكومة جمهورية كوريا في مناسبات سابقة موقفها بشأن انضمام جمهوريــة
كوريا الى عضوية الامم المتحدة لاسيما عزمها على أن تسعى الى الانضمام الى عضويــة
الامم المتحدة في خلال هذه السنة .

وجمهورية كوريا بوصفها دولة محبة للسلم وراغبة وقادرة على تنفيذ جميـــع
الالتزامات الواردة في ميثاق الامم المتحدة مؤهلة تماما لعضوية الامم المتحــــدة .
وبوصفها بلدا له علاقات دبلوماسية عالمية تقريبا ، وبوصفها الدولة الثانية عشرة في
العالـم من حيث حجم تجارتها فإنها على استعداد للإسهام على النحو المناسب في أعمــال
الامم المتحدة بوصفها عضوا كامل العضوية وبصورة تتناسب مع مركزها في المجتمـــع
الدولي .

ويقضي مبدأ العالمية ، الذي تحرص عليه الامم المتحدة ، بقبول انضمام جميـــع
من يرغب في الانضمام إلى الامم المتحدة من الدول ذات السيادة والأهلية للعضويـــة .
ويكتسب هذا المبدأ أهمية أكبر عن ذي قبل مع قيام الامم المتحدة بدور متزايد الأهميـة
في عصر ما بعد الحرب الباردة . وإن ما يجري في الساحة السياسية الدولية من تغيرات
لم يسبق لها مثيل وتنطوي على روح تصالح وتعاون جديدة يدعو إلى حل مسألة عضويــة
كوريا التي طال أمدها .

وكما بُيّن ببلاغة في السنة الماضية في خلال المناقشة العامة في الـــدورة
الخامسة والأربعين للجمعية العامة أصبح المجتمع الدولي يشعر بأنه ينبغي قبـــول
انضمام جمهورية كوريا إلى عضوية الامم المتحدة دون مزيد من الإبطاء .

وإن جمهورية كوريا في سعيها إلى الانضمام إلى عضوية الامم المتحدة تكـــرر
الاعراب عن أملها الكبير في أن تنضم جمهورية كوريا الديمقراطية الشعبية أيضا إلـــى
عضوية الامم المتحدة إما في نفس الوقت مع الجنوب أو في الوقت الذي يراه الشمـــال
مناسبا . وتعيد جمهورية كوريا الاعراب عن موقفها المتمثل في ترحيبها بانضمـــام
جمهورية كوريا الديمقراطية الشعبية إلى عضوية الامم المتحدة .

../..   ت.٥٧٧(٩١)

                        25-23

                                                              0106

علاوة على ذلك ترى جمهورية كوريا أن العضوية المتوازية لكـل من جمهوريتـي كوريا في الامم المتحدة ليس فيه أي مساس بالغاية النهائية المتمثلة في توحيـد كوريا . فينبغي أن تعتبر العضوية المتوازية إجراءً قويا لبناء الثقة بقدر ما تمثـل التزامـا راسخا من جانب كلتـا جمهوريتي كوريا بأحكام ميثاق الامم المتحدة ومبادئه .

إن توحيد ألمانيا الشرقية وألمانيـا الغربيـة واليمن الشمالية واليمـن الجنوبيـة ، التي كان منها لكل عضوية مستقلة في الامم المتحدة يبرر هذا الرأي ويدحض ما يُزعم من أن عضوية الامم المتحدة قد تديم الانقسام القومي لكوريا أو تضفي عليـه الشرعية ، الامر الذي من شأنه أن يعرقل الجهود الرامية إلى توحيد كوريا .

والواقع هو أن المجتمع الدولي قد اعترف منذ أمد طويل بوجود كوريا الشماليـة وكوريا الجنوبية في شبه الجزيرة الكورية . ولجمهورية كوريا وجمهوريـة كوريـا الديمقراطية الشعبية علاقات دبلوماسيـة بـ ١٤٨ بلدا و ١٠٥ بلدان ، على التوالـي . ولتسعين بلدا من هذه البلدان علاقات دبلوماسية مع كل من البلدين . ولكل مـن جمهوريتي كوريا عضوية مستقلة في معظم المنظمات الحكومية الدولية ، بما في ذلك الوكالات المتخصصة التابعة للامم المتحدة . وعلى هذا النحو فإن عضوية كوريا في الامـم المتحدة سواءً كانت مستقلة أو متزامنة ستكون أمرا منطقيا ملازما للواقع السياسـي الدولي .

ولقد بذلت جمهورية كوريا كل ما في وسعها وبحسن نية للانضمام إلى عضوية الامم المتحدة مع جمهورية كوريا الديمقراطية الشعبية في خلال هذه السنة برغبة خالصة فـي أن تسهم العضوية في الامم المتحدة في عملية تصالح كوريا وتوحيدها وتعزز أيضا السلـم والامن في شبه الجزيرة الكورية ، لكنها لم تنجح في ذلك .

وعلى الرغم من هذه الجهود تمسكت جمهورية كوريا الديمقراطية الشعبية بصيغـة "العضوية الواحدة" وهي ليست غير عملية فحسب وإنما تتعارض أيضا مع أحكام ميثـاق الامم المتحدة وممارسات الامم المتحدة ووكالاتها المتخصصة . وإن عدم تأييد الـدول الاعضاء في الامم المتحدة لهذه الصيغة في خلال المناقشة العامة في العام الماضي يعبـر عن عدم موافقتها على صيغة كوريا الشمالية .

إن حكومة جمهورية كوريا ما زالت تأمل في انضمام كل من جمهوريتي كوريا إلـى العضوية في خلال هذه السنة . بيد أنه إذا ظلت جمهورية كوريا الديمقراطية الشعبيـة

.. /..   ٥٧٧.ن(٩١)

25-24

0107

S/22455
Arabic   -o-
Page 5

على معارضتها لهذا الخيار ، واختارت لأي سبب من الاسباب الا تنضم إلى الأمم المتحدة ،
فإن جمهورية كوريا ، ممارسة منها لحقها السيادي ، ستتخذ الخطوة اللازمة للانضمام
إلى العضوية قبل افتتاح الدورة السادسة والأربعين للجمعية العامة .

وإن حكومة جمهورية كوريا على اقتناع بأن جمهورية كوريا بالتأييد الساحق من
جانب الدول الأعضاء في الأمم المتحدة لقضية عضويتها المشروعة ستتمكن في الأشهر
القادمة من أن تحتل مكانها الشرعي في الأمم المتحدة .

- - - - -

(٩١)ف٠٥٧٧

25-25

WJAM-0015 외 별지참조
WJAM-0015 910408 1813 FL

WHK -0551 WSN -0098 WKA -0074 WUSM-0026 WCNM-0011

WSO -0075 WBC -0039 WBE -0576 WFK -0212 WLP -0039
                          WNM -166

WHM -0085 WJD -0154

0103

발 신 전 보

분류번호	보존기간

번 호 : WJAM-0015 외 별지참조   종별 : _____

수 신 : 주 수신처 참조   대사. 총영사/

발 신 : 장 관 (국연)

제 목 : 유연가입에 관한 정부각서

　

1. 유연가입문제에 관한 아국입장과 금년중 가입실현 의지를 밝힌 정부각서 (91.4.5.자)를 별첨 타전하니, 귀지에서도 우리의 유연가입 홍보에 적의 활용바람.

2. 상기 각서는 금주초 유연안보리문서로 유연전회원국에 배포될 예정임.

첨 부 : 동 각서 (영문) 1부.   끝.

(국제기구조약국장 문동석)

수신처 : 일본지역(WJAM : 일본제외), 아주지역(홍콩, 시드니, 카라치)
미주지역 (WUSM : 미국, 유연 제외), 카나다지역(WCNM : 카나다 제외),
남미지역 (쌍파울로 총영사관),
구주지역 (바르셀로나, 백림, 프랑크푸르트, 라스팔마스, 함부르크),
중동지역 (젯다)

보안통제	〜

앙고재	년4월8일	유엔과	기안자성명 여	과 장 〜	국 장	차 관	장 관 〜	외신과통제

<u>MEMORANDUM OF THE GOVERNMENT OF THE REPUBLIC OF KOREA</u>

5 April 1991

The Government of the Republic of Korea has made clear on previous occasions its position concerning membership of the Republic of Korea in the United Nations, particularly its determination to seek United Nations membership during the course of this year.

The Republic of Korea, as a peace-loving state willing and able to carry out all obligations set forth in the United Nations Charter, is fully qualified for membership in the United Nations. As a country which maintains almost universal diplomatic relations and as the world's twelfth largest trading nation, it is ready to make its due contribution to the work of the United Nations as a full Member and in a manner commensurate with its standing in the international community.

The principle of universality cherished by the United Nations requires the admission of all eligible sovereign states that wish to join the United Nations. This principle gains more relevance than ever as the United Nations assumes an increasingly vital role in the post-Cold War era. The unprecedented changes taking place in the international political environment, featuring a new spirit of reconciliation and cooperation, call for the resolution of Korea's membership question at long last.

As was eloquently manifested last year during the general debate of the 45th session of the General Assembly, it has become the sense of the international community that the admission of the Republic of Korea to United Nations membership should be realized without further delay.

/...

-1-

0111

In seeking United Nations membership, the Republic of Korea reiterates its earnest hope that the Democratic People's Republic of Korea(DPRK) will also join the United Nations, either together with the South, or at the time the North deems appropriate. The Republic of Korea restates its position that it would welcome DPRK's membership.

Furthermore, the Republic of Korea holds the view that the parallel membership of both Koreas in the United Nations is entirely without prejudice to the ultimate objective of Korea's reunification. Parallel membership should constitute a powerful confidence building measure insofar as it will represent a firm commitment of both Koreas to the' provisions and principles of the United Nations Charter.

The unification of East and West Germany and of North and South Yemen, each of which had maintained separate membership in the United Nations, validates this view and disproves the contention that United Nations membership might serve to perpetuate or legitimize Korea's national division, thus hindering efforts for Korea's reunification.

It is a matter of fact that the international community has long recognized the existence of South and North Korea on the Korean Peninsula. In reality, the Republic of Korea and the DPRK maintain diplomatic relations with 146 and 105 countries respectively. Ninety of these countries maintain concurrent diplomatic relations with both. Each also has separate membership in most inter-governmental organizations, including specialized agencies of the United Nations. Thus, Korea's United Nations membership, separate or simultaneous, will be a logical corollary of the international political reality.

/...

-2-

In the sincere belief that United Nations membership will contribute to the process of Korean reconciliation and reunification, as well as enhance peace and security on the Korean Peninsula, the Republic of Korea has made every effort in good faith to join the United Nations together with the DPRK during the course of last year, but without success.

Despite these efforts, however, the DPRK has adhered to the 'single-seat membership' formula which is not only infeasible but runs counter to the provisions of the United Nations Charter and the practices followed by the United Nations and its specialized agenices. The lack of support from the United Nations Member States with respect to this formula during the general debate last year reflects their disapproval of the North Korean formula.

The Government of the Republic of Korea remains hopeful of realizing membership of both Koreas during the course of this year. However, if the DPRK continues to oppose this option and for any reason chooses not to join the United Nations, the Republic of Korea, exercising its sovereign right, will take the necessary step toward its membership before the opening of the 46th session of the General Assembly.

The Government of the Republic of Korea is convinced that, with the overwhelming support of the Member States of the United Nations for the legitimate cause of its membership, the Republic of Korea will be able to assume its rightful place in the United Nations in the months ahead.

- - - - -

-3-

0113

발 신 전 보

번   호 : WUN-0795   910408 1933 FJ 종별 : ＿＿＿＿

수   신 : 주 유엔   대사. /총영사

발   신 : 장 관 (국연)

제   목 : 메모랜덤

연 : WUN-0750

유엔가입에 관한 아국 메모랜덤의 불어.서반아어판 안보리문서 배포

즉시 FAX 편 송부바람.   끝.

(국제기구조약국장   문동석)

보안통제	Uy

앙고재	91년 4월 8일	기안자 성명	과 장	국 장	차 관	장 관
	42과					

외신과통제

0114

분류번호	보존기간

발 신 전 보

번   호 :   WUK-0651   910408 1938 FJ   종별 :

수   신 : 주 영 국   대사. 총영사// (조상훈 참사관님)

발   신 : 장 관   (이규형 배상)

제   목 :   업 연

1. 제번하옵고, 메모랜덤 관련, 주재국측이 먼저 알고 언급케 되어 죄송함. 뉴욕에서 4.5. CG 구성국들에게 설명한 바 있었으며, 본부로서는 동일 EM 타전 코자 한 바 있으나, 결재과정에서 하루 지연케 되었음.

2. AI건 관련 당시 최대사대리께서 잘 해주시어 감사드림. 일전 황서기관 접촉상황도 포함하여 상부 보고하였는 바, 잘 대응하고 있다는 평가가 있었다고 함. 문재점은 잘 알고 있으나, 현실적인 고려하에서 AI측에 대한 주기적인 접촉 및 우리입장 설명등의 활동이 필요함. 혜량하여 주시기 바람.

3. 건안하시기 기원하오며,   끝.

예 고 | 一독후파기 파. 1`8° . . | [서명]

보 안 통 제	[서명]

0115

─── ─ ─청와대보고─

유엔加入에 관한 政府覺書 配布

1991. 4. 9.

外 務 部

> 유엔加入에 관한 政府覺書(1991.4.5.자)가 유엔安保理
> 文書로 配布된 것과 關聯, 그간 當部의 弘報措置事項 및
> 今後 推進計劃을 아래 報告드립니다.

1. 國内 弘報措置事項

    o 外務長官, MBC 라디오 '뉴스의 광장' 出演 説明

    o 次官, 1次官補, 擔當局長, 公報官등 外務部 幹部,
       主要 日刊紙 主筆, 論説委員등 接觸, 政府立場 説明
       및 協調 要請

    * 其他 弘報活動
       - 國内言論에 覺書配布 관련 報道資料 事前 傳達 (4.6)
       - 外交政策諮問委員을 對象으로 覺書提出 背景 및 意義
         説明 (4.6)
       - 國會 外務統一委員會 委員에게 覺書 및 報道資料
         傳達 (4.8)

0116

2. 言論報道 內容分析

言論報道 現況 (4.8-4.9)

---

o 全 日刊紙 1면 톱 또는 中間 톱기사로 揭載
o 東亞.韓國日報등 8個 日刊紙 政府立場 支持 社說 揭載
o 外國言論
  - 유엔加入에 관한 我國立場 및 今年中 加入 實現意志
    說明
  - 北韓主張 및 單一議席加入案의 問題點 紹介
  - 問題解決의 關鍵인 中國의 態度 不確實

國內言論 社說論旨

---

o 晚時之歎의 感이 있으며 早速히 加入 實現되어야 함.
o 北韓은 非現實的 主張을 버리고 우리와 함께 유엔에
  加入해야 함.
o 覺書 提出은 今年中 유엔加入 實現이라는 政府의
  결연한 意志 表現 및 加入을 위한 公式行動 開始
  意味
o 中國의 建設的 役割 促求

0117

3. 向後推進計劃

主要 着眼點

o 主要言論 社説에서 政府立場에 대한 支持 輿論이 高潮된
  점을 勘案, 輿論形成層 對象 説明活動 強化
o 海外支持 輿論造成에 力點
  - 在外公館에서 現地言論 接觸強化 및 國內循環 弘報展開
o 野黨을 包含한 主要 政黨人士에 대한 政府立場 説明
  * 박정수 國會外務統一委員長을 爲始, 문동환, 조순승
    議員등 10名에 대한 説明 旣措置
o 海外出張 政府高位人士에 대한 유엔加入問題에 대한
  政府立場 説明

細部施行計劃

o '外交問題解説' 作成 配布
  - '유엔加入' 主題下의 説明資料 作成, 輿論 形成層
    6,000餘名을 對象으로 송부
o 公職者 對象 政府立場 説明
  - IPU 평양總會(4.29-5.4) 參加 代表團
  - 對外政策研究班(PSG) 委員
  - 國際法 및 國際政治 專攻 大學教授등
o 外交安保研究院과 地方 大學과의 세미나 活用

- 끝 -

0118

0119

발 신 전 보

	분류번호	보존기간

번   호 :   WUN-0822   910409 1803   FL   종별 :

수   신 :   주   유엔   대사. ♣♣♣♣♣♣아

발   신 :   장   관   (국연)

제   목 :   안보리 문서 배포

                대 : UNW-0834

대호 배포된 각서를 파편으로 2부씩 송부바람.   끝.

                                            (국제기구조약국장 문동석)

0121

WAG-0158   910409 1812   FN

WMO -0105   WMT -0062   WTN -0092   WCM -0079   WIV -0105

WGA -0043   WSL -0124   WZR -0096   WHA -0056   WBB -0159

WFR -0717

발 신 전 보

분류번호	보존기간

번 호 : WAG-0158 외 별지참조   종별 : 2/30

수 신 : 주   수신처 참조 대사.♣♣♥♣♥♣아

발 신 : 장 관   (국연)

제 목 : 불어본 각서 송부

연 : EM-0011

별첨

연호 유엔안보리 문서로 배포된 각서를 타전하니 적의 활용바람. 끝.

첨부 : 상기 각서 (불어본)

수신처 : 주알제리, 모로코, 모리타니아, 튀니지,
가
께메룬, 코트디봐르, 가봉, 세네갈, 자이르,

아이티, 벨지움, 프랑스대사

보안통제	4y.

앙고재	년4월수일	기안자성명		과 장	국 장	차 관	장 관	외신과통제
		유엔과	어	4y.			ん	

0122

WAR-0149

0123

WAR-0149 외 별지참조

WAR-0149 910409 1821 FN

WBV -0084 WBR -0165 WCS -0091 WCL -0074 WCO -0069
WEQ -0068 WGU -0079 WMX -0204 WPU -0148 WUR -0050
WPG -0094 WVZ -0098 WSP -0178

발 신 전 보

	분류번호	보존기간

번 호 : WAR-0149 외 별지참조 종별 : 2131

수 신 : 주 수신처 참조 대사. ♣♣♣♣♣아

발 신 : 장 관 (국연)

제 목 : 서반어본 각서 송부

연 : EM-0011

연호 유엔안보리 문서로 배포된 서반어본 각서를 별첨 타전하니
적의 활용바람. 끝.

첨 부 : 상기 각서 (서반어본)

수신처 : 주아르젠틴, 볼리비아, 브라질, 칠레, 콜롬비아,
코스타리카, 에쿠아돌, 과테말라, 혼두라스,
멕시코, 파라과이, 페루, 우루과이, 베네주엘라,
스페인대사

앙고재	년4월9일	기안자성명 유엔과 여	과 장	국 장	차 관 장 관	보안통제
						외신과통제

0124

유엔加入問題에 관한 政府覺書

(91.4.11. PSG 會議資料)

91. 4. 10.
國際聯合課

1. 政府覺書 配布

    ○ 政府는 유엔加入問題에 관한 우리의 立場을 종합적으로 說明하고 今年中
    유엔加入을 實現하고자 하는 意志를 밝히는 91.4.5字 覺書를 유엔安保理에
    提出하여 同 覺書가 安保理 文書로 91.4.8. 유엔 全會員國에 配布됨.

2. 政府覺書 主要要旨

    ○ 우리는 유엔會員國 資格을 完全히 갖추고 있으며; 유엔의 活動에 會員國
    으로서 積極 參與하길 希望함.

    ○ 우리는 北韓이 우리와 함께 유엔에 加入토록 지난해동안 努力하였으나
    北韓은 現實 不可能한 單一議席 加入案을 固執하고 있음.

    ○ 南北韓 유엔同時加入을 希望하는 우리의 立場에는 변함이 없으나, 北韓이
    이에 繼續 反對하거나, 加入치 않기로 決定하는 境遇, 우리는 今年中
    우리의 유엔加入 實現을 위한 必要한 措置를 취할 것임.

3. 유엔加入 支持交涉

    ○ 安保理文書 配布 以前,

    - 유엔代表部에서 主要友邦國, 安保理理事國 및 主要 유엔會員國에
    上記 覺書를 傳達하고 我國 유엔加入 支持交涉 施行

    - 유엔駐在 中國, 蘇聯의 關係官을 接觸, 覺書 內容을 說明하고 覺書 傳達

    ○ 유엔事務總長 및 安保理 非常任理事國 外務長官 앞으로 同 覺書 內容을
    中心으로 我國立場을 說明하는 外務長官 書翰 發送中

    ○ 駐韓外交使節앞 公翰添附, 同 覺書 配布

0125

4. 弘報活動

　가. 國內 弘報措置事項

　　　o 外務長官, MBC 라디오 "뉴스의 광장" 出演 説明

　　　o 次官, 1次官補, 擔當局長, 公報官등 外務部 幹部, 主要 日刊紙 主筆,
　　　　論説委員등 接觸, 政府立場 説明 및 協調 要請

　　　* 其他 弘報活動

　　　　- 國內言論에 覺書配布 관련 報道資料 事前 傳達 (4.6)

　　　　- 外交政策諮問委員을 對象으로 覺書提出 背景 및 意義 説明 (4.6)

　　　　- 國會 外務統一委員會 委員에게 覺書 및 報道資料 傳達 (4.8)

　나. 海外 弘報措置事項

　　　o 유엔大使, 유엔駐在 外信記者團에 覺書 説明 및 傳達

　　　o 全在外公館, 駐在國 言論對象 弘報活動 展開

　다. 言論報道 內容分析

　　1) 言論報道 現況 (4.8-4.10)

　　　o 全 日刊紙 1면 톱 또는 中間 톱기사로 揭載

　　　o 東亞.韓國日報등 10個 日刊紙 政府立場 支持 社説 揭載

　　　o 外國言論

　　　　- 유엔加入에 관한 我國立場 및 今年中 加入 實現意志 説明

　　　　- 北韓主張 및 單一議席加入案의 問題點 紹介

　　　　- 問題解決의 關鍵인 中國의 態度 不確實

　　2) 國內言論 社説論旨

　　　o 晚時之歎의 感이 있으며 早速히 加入 實現되어야 함.

　　　o 北韓은 非現實的 主張을 버리고 우리와 함께 유엔에 加入해야 함.

　　　o 覺書 提出은 今年中 유엔加入 實現이라는 政府의 결연한 意志 表現
　　　　및 加入을 위한 公式行動 開始 意味

0126

o 中國의 建設的 役割 促求

* 단, 한겨레新聞은 南北高位級會談 進展에 優先 힘 쏟아야 한다는
  內容의 社說 揭載

나. 向後 推進計劃

o '外交問題解說' 作成 配布

  - '유엔加入' 主題下의 說明資料 作成, 輿論 形成層 6,000餘名을
    對象으로 송부

o 公職者 對象 政府立場 說明

  - IPU 평양總會(4.29-5.4) 參加 代表團

  - 國際法 및 國際政治 專攻 大學敎授등

o 外交安保硏究院과 地方 大學과의 세미나 活用

0127

EMBASSY OF TUNISIA

SEOUL

No.276/91/Pol.

Seoul, April 10, 1991

The Embassy of Tunisia presents its compliments to the Ministry of Foreign Affairs and has the honour to acknowledge receipt of its Note OGO 91-233 of April 8, 1991 enclosing a memorandum of the Government of the Republic of Korea concerning its United Nations membership, the contents of which have been duly noted.

The Embassy of Tunisia informs the Ministry that the above mentioned Note has been forwarded to the proper authorities in Tunis for favorable consideration.

The Embassy of Tunisia avails itself of this opportunity to renew to the Ministry the assurances of its highest consideration.

Ministry of Foreign Affairs
77-6, Sejong-ro, Chongro-ku
Seoul

0128

주 국 련 대 표 부

주국련 20312-
수신 장관 **249**

참조 국제기구조약국장

제목 안보리 문서 송부

        연 : UNW-0834

        대 : WUN-0822

1991. 4. 12.

연호 안보리 문서 6개국어본 각 2부씩을 별첨 송부합니다.

첨 부 : 상기 문서 각 2부.   끝.

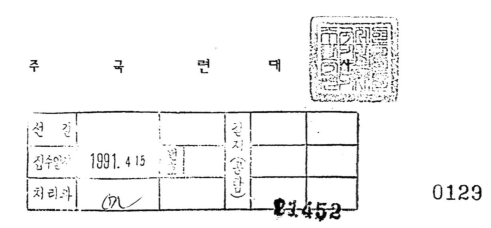

0129

Conseil de sécurité

Distr.
GENERALE

S/22455*
9 avril 1991
FRANCAIS
ORIGINAL : ANGLAIS

NOTE DU PRESIDENT DU CONSEIL DE SECURITE

La lettre jointe, datée du 5 avril 1991, a été adressée au Président du Conseil de sécurité par l'Observateur permanent de la République de Corée auprès de l'Organisation des Nations Unies. Conformément à la demande qui y est formulée, elle est distribuée en tant que document du Conseil de sécurité.

---

* Nouveau tirage pour raisons techniques.

91-11415   5201T   (F)

/...

0130

ANNEXE

Lettre datée du 5 avril 1991, adressée au Président du Conseil de
sécurité par l'Observateur permanent de la République de Corée
auprès de l'Organisation des Nations Unies

D'ordre de mon gouvernement, j'ai l'honneur de vous faire tenir ci-joint un
mémorandum du Gouvernement de la République de Corée concernant son admission à
l'Organisation des Nations Unies.

Je vous serais très obligé de bien vouloir faire distribuer le texte de la
présente lettre et du mémorandum joint comme document du Conseil de sécurité.

L'Ambassadeur

(Signé) Chang Hee ROE

0131 /...

PIECE JOINTE

Mémorandum du Gouvernement de la République de Corée

Le Gouvernement de la République de Corée a déjà, à plusieurs occasions, précisé sa position concernant l'admission de la République de Corée à l'Organisation des Nations Unies, et en particulier sa volonté de demander cette admission cette année.

La République de Corée, Etat épris de paix, désireux et capable d'assumer toutes les obligations énoncées dans la Charte des Nations Unies, a pleinement qualité pour être admise à l'ONU. Elle entretient des relations diplomatiques avec la quasi universalité des pays et occupe le douzième rang dans le commerce mondial, et elle est disposée à apporter à l'action de l'ONU la contribution qu'on peut attendre d'elle en tant que membre à part entière, et à la mesure de sa position dans la communauté internationale.

Le principe d'universalité auquel souscrit l'Organisation a pour corollaire l'obligation d'y admettre tous les Etats souverains qui souhaitent y entrer et réunissent les conditions voulues. Ce principe est plus valable que jamais au moment où l'Organisation assume un rôle de plus en plus décisif au lendemain de la guerre froide. Les changements inouïs qui se produisent dans le climat politique international, et qui marquent l'avènement d'un nouvel esprit de réconciliation et de coopération, invitent à régler enfin la question de l'admission de la Corée.

Comme l'a éloquemment montré, l'an dernier, le débat général de la quarante-cinquième session de l'Assemblée générale, la communauté internationale a maintenant le sentiment que l'entrée de la République de Corée à l'ONU ne peut plus être différée.

En demandant son admission à l'Organisation des Nations Unies, la République de Corée réitère son espoir sincère que la République populaire démocratique de Corée (RPDC) entrera également à l'ONU, soit au même moment que le Sud, soit quand le Nord le jugera opportun. La République de Corée réaffirme sa position, à savoir qu'elle saluerait l'admission de la RPDC.

En outre, la République de Corée estime que l'admission parallèle des deux Corée à l'ONU ne préjuge en rien la question de l'objectif ultime qu'est la réunification du pays. La présence simultanée des deux Corée à l'ONU constituerait une puissante mesure de renforcement de la confiance, car elle témoignerait de la ferme volonté des deux Corée de se conformer aux dispositions et aux principes de la Charte des Nations Unies.

L'unification de l'Allemagne de l'Est et de l'Ouest et du Yémen du Nord et du Sud, qui précédemment occupaient chacun un siège à l'ONU, conforte cette façon de voir et réfute l'idée que l'admission à l'Organisation des Nations Unies pourrait avoir pour effet de perpétuer ou de légitimer la division de la nation coréenne et risquerait par-là d'entraver les efforts de réunification.

0132   /...

La communauté internationale a, en vérité, admis depuis longtemps l'existence dans la péninsule coréenne d'une Corée du Sud et d'une Corée du Nord. Le fait est que la République de Corée et la RPDC entretiennent respectivement des relations diplomatiques avec 148 et 105 pays. Quatre-vingt-dix de ces pays entretiennent simultanément des relations diplomatiques avec l'une et l'autre. Chacune des deux a été admise séparément dans la plupart des organisations intergouvernementales, y compris certaines institutions spécialisées de l'ONU. Ainsi l'admission séparée ou simultanée des deux Corée à l'Organisation des Nations Unies serait le corollaire logique de la situation politique internationale réelle.

Sincèrement convaincue que l'admission de la République de Corée à l'Organisation des Nations Unies contribuerait à la réconciliation en Corée et à la réunification du pays et servirait la cause de la paix et de la sécurité dans la péninsule, la République de Corée, en toute bonne foi, n'a épargné aucun effort pour entrer à l'ONU, avec la RPDC, l'an dernier, mais sans succès.

En dépit de ces efforts, pourtant, la RPDC s'en tient à la formule "du siège unique" qui non seulement ne peut fonctionner, mais est contraire aux dispositions de la Charte des Nations Unies et à la pratique suivie par l'ONU et par ses institutions spécialisées. Le fait que les Etats Membres de l'ONU n'ont pas repris cette formule à leur compte, pendant le débat général, l'an dernier, porte témoignage de leur désapprobation de la formule nord-coréenne.

Le Gouvernement de la République de Corée continue à espérer que les deux Corée seront admises à l'ONU cette année. Cependant, si la RPDC continue à s'opposer à cette solution, et, pour une raison quelconque, décide de ne pas entrer à l'ONU, la République de Corée, exerçant les droits afférents à sa souveraineté, fera ce qu'il faudra pour devenir un Etat Membre avant l'ouverture de la quarante-sixième session de l'Assemblée générale.

Le Gouvernement de la République de Corée est convaincu que, forte du soutien massif des Etats Membres pour le principe légitime de son admission, la République de Corée pourra dans les mois qui viennent prendre la place qui lui revient au sein des Nations Unies.

0133

NACIONES UNIDAS

Consejo de Seguridad

Distr.
GENERAL

S/22455
5 de abril de 1991
ESPAÑOL
ORIGINAL: INGLES

NOTA DEL PRESIDENTE DEL CONSEJO DE SEGURIDAD

La carta de fecha 5 de abril de 1991 que figura en el anexo fue dirigida al Presidente del Consejo de Seguridad por el Observador Permanente de la República de Corea ante las Naciones Unidas. Conforme a lo solicitado, se procede a su distribución como documento del Consejo de Seguridad.

91-11150   2088a

/...

0134

ANEXO

<u>Carta de fecha 5 de abril de 1991 dirigida al Presidente del Consejo
de Seguridad por el Observador Permanente de la República de Corea
ante las Naciones Unidas</u>

Siguiendo instrucciones de mi Gobierno, tengo el honor de transmitirle un memorando del Gobierno de la República de Corea relativo a su admisión en las Naciones Unidas.

Le agradecería que tuviera a bien hacer distribuir el texto de la presente carta y el memorando adjunto como documento del Consejo de Seguridad.

(<u>Firmado</u>)   Chang Hee ROE
Embajador

/...

0135

APENDICE

Memorando del Gobierno de la República de Corea

El Gobierno de la República de Corea ha expresado claramente en ocasiones anteriores su posición con respecto a la admisión en las Naciones Unidas, y, en particular, su determinación de solicitarla en el curso del presente año.

La República de Corea, que es un Estado pacífico, deseoso de cumplir todas las obligaciones enunciadas en la Carta de las Naciones Unidas y capaz de hacerlo, reúne todas las condiciones necesarias para ser Miembro de las Naciones Unidas. Tratándose de un país que mantiene relaciones diplomáticas casi universales y ocupa el duodécimo lugar mundial en cuanto a volumen comercial, la República de Corea está dispuesta a contribuir debidamente a la labor de las Naciones Unidas como Miembro pleno y de forma consecuente con su posición en la comunidad internacional.

El principio de universalidad consagrado por las Naciones Unidas impone la admisión de todos los Estados soberanos que reúnan las condiciones necesarias y deseen pertenecer a la Organización. Este principio cobra más importancia que nunca en momentos en que las Naciones Unidas asumen un papel cada vez más vital en la era posterior a la guerra fría. Los cambios sin precedentes que tienen lugar en las circunstancias políticas internacionales, y que revelan un nuevo espíritu de reconciliación y de cooperación, exigen que se decida por fin la cuestión del ingreso de Corea.

Como se manifestó elocuentemente el año pasado durante el debate general del cuadragésimo quinto período de sesiones de la Asamblea, la comunidad internacional ha tomado conciencia de que la República de Corea debe ser admitida sin más demora en las Naciones Unidas.

Al aspirar a la condición de Miembro de las Naciones Unidas, la República de Corea reitera su ferviente esperanza de que la República Popular Democrática de Corea (RPDC) también ingrese a las Naciones Unidas, ya bien junto con el Sur, o en el momento en que el Norte lo estime apropiado. La República de Corea declara una vez más su posición de que acogerá con agrado la admisión de la RPDC.

Además, en opinión de la República de Corea, la presencia simultánea de las dos Coreas en las Naciones Unidas no menoscaba en modo alguno el objetivo último de su reunificación. La presencia simultánea debería constituir una poderosa medida de fomento de la confianza por cuanto representará la firme adhesión de los dos Estados a las disposiciones y los principios de la Carta de las Naciones Unidas.

La unificación de Alemania Oriental y Alemania Occidental y del Yemen del Norte y del Sur, cada uno de los cuales fue Miembro de las Naciones Unidas por separado, confiere validez a esta opinión y refuta el argumento de que la admisión en las Naciones Unidas podría servir para perpetuar o legitimar la división nacional de Corea, y obstaculizar así los esfuerzos en pro de su reunificación.

/...

0136

La realidad es que la comunidad internacional reconoció hace tiempo la
existencia de Corea del Sur y Corea del Norte en la misma península. De hecho, la
República de Corea y la RPDC mantienen relaciones diplomáticas con 148 y 105 países
respectivamente, y 90 de esos países mantienen relaciones diplomáticas con ambas.
Asimismo, cada una de ellas es, por separado, miembro de la mayor parte de las
organizaciones intergubernamentales, incluidos los organismos especializados de las
Naciones Unidas. Por ende, la admisión de Corea en las Naciones Unidas, ya sea por
separado o de forma simultánea, será el corolario lógico de la realidad política
internacional.

La República de Corea está sinceramente convencida de que el ingreso en las
Naciones Unidas contribuirá al proceso de reconciliación y reunificación de Corea y
a la vez promoverá la paz y la seguridad en la península de Corea. En
consecuencia, durante el pasado año, hizo de buena fe cuanto estuvo a su alcance
por incorporarse a las Naciones Unidas junto con la RPDC. Lamentablemente sus
gestiones resultaron infructuosas.

En cambio, la RPDC es partidaria del ingreso de una sola representación,
fórmula que no sólo es impracticable, sino que además atenta contra las
disposiciones de la Carta de las Naciones Unidas y contra las prácticas de la
Organización y sus organismos especializados. La falta de apoyo de los Estados
Miembros de las Naciones Unidas durante el debate general celebrado el año pasado
demuestra que no aprueban la fórmula de Corea del Norte.

El Gobierno de la República de Corea mantiene la esperanza de que las dos
Coreas sean admitidas el presente año. Ahora bien, si la RPDC se sigue oponiendo a
esta opción, y por cualquier motivo decide no incorporarse a las Naciones Unidas,
la República de Corea, en ejercicio de su derecho soberano, hará las gestiones
necesarias para ser admitida antes de la inauguración del cuadragésimo sexto
período de sesiones de la Asamblea General.

El Gobierno de la República de Corea está persuadido de que, al contar con el
abrumador apoyo de los Estados Miembros de las Naciones Unidas a la legítima causa
de su admisión, en los meses venideros la República de Corea podrá ocupar el lugar
que legítimamente le corresponde en las Naciones Unidas.

0137

联合国

安全理事会

S

Distr.
GENERAL

S/22455
5 April 1991
CHINESE
ORIGINAL：ENGLISH

安全理事会主席的说明

所附为1991年4月5日大韩民国常驻联合国观察员给联合国安全理事会主席的信。兹依照信内要求，将此信作为安全理事会的文件散发。

91-11146

0138

附 件

1991年4月5日
大韩民国常驻联合国观察员
给安全理事会主席的信

奉我国政府指示,谨转递大韩民国政府关于其联合国会员籍的备忘录。
谨请将本信全文及所附备忘录作为安全理事会文件散发为荷。

大使
卢昌熹(签名)

0139

附　文

大韩民国政府备忘录

　　大韩民国政府在过去已在许多场合表明其对于大韩民国在联合国会籍所持的立场,特别是关于大韩民国在本年内争取联合国会员籍的决心。

　　大韩民国,作为一个愿意且能够履行《联合国宪章》规定的一切义务的爱好和平的国家,完全有资格成为联合国的会员国。作为与全世界几乎所有的国家都维持外交关系的,世界第十二大贸易国,大韩民国已准备好愿以联合国充分会员身份与在国际社会所处地位相衬的方式对联合国的工作作出应有的贡献。

　　联合国所重视的普遍性原则要求允许希望加入联合国的一切有资格的主权国家都加入联合国。随着联合国在冷战后的时代承担日益重要的角色,这个普遍性原则比以往任何时候更显得重要。国际政治环境里发生的以和解与合作的新精神为特点的史无前例的变化,终于要求解决韩国会员籍的问题。

　　正如去年大会第四十五届会议一般性辩论中令人信服地显示的,整个国际社会都感觉到,不应该再拖延实现大韩民国加入联合国了。

　　大韩民国在争取加入为联合国会员国时,重申其热切盼望朝鲜民主主义人民共和国(北朝鲜)也与南韩同时,或在北朝鲜认为适当的时候,加入联合国。大韩民国重申它欢迎北朝鲜加入联合国的立场。

　　此外,大韩民国始终认为两韩在联合国内的平行会员籍是完全不影响韩国统一的最终目标的。平行会员籍,只要它代表两韩对《联合国宪章》的规定和原则的坚定承诺,就应该是一项有力的建立信心的措施。

　　东西德国和南北也门两国在联合国中都曾保持过分开的会员籍。这两国的统一支持了此一意见而否定了联合国会员籍可能会延续或使韩国的民族分裂合法化从而阻碍了韩国统一努力的说法。

0140

实际上国际社会早已承认了韩国半岛上南北韩的存在。事实是,大韩民国与北朝鲜分别与148和105个国家保持外交关系。九十个国家与两边都保持并行的外交关系。南北双方也分别在大多数政府间组织,包括联合国专门机构享有会员籍。因此,韩国的联合国会员籍,不论分开的或并存的,都将是国际政治现实的逻辑必然结果。

去年,大韩民国由于真心相信联合国会员籍会有助于韩国和解与统一的进程,以及增进韩国半岛的和平与安全,所以诚意地作出一切努力,争取同北朝鲜一道加入联合国,但未成功。

然而,尽管这样的努力,北朝鲜还是坚守"单一会员国席位"的方式,这不仅是行不通,并且与《联合国宪章》的规定和联合国及其专门机构采取的作法背道而驰。去年一般辩论期间,联合国会员国对这一方式缺乏支持反映了它们对这一北朝鲜方式的不赞同。

大韩民国政府仍然希望今年内韩国两方的会员籍能够实现。然而,如果北朝鲜继续反对这一备选办法,并且不论用任何理由而选择不加入联合国,则大韩民国将行使其主权权利,在大会第四十六届会议开幕前采取为取得会员籍的必要步骤。

大韩民国政府深信,在联合国会员国对其争取会员籍的正当事业的绝大多数支持下,几个月后大韩民国将能够取得其在联合国的正当地位。

- - - - -

0141

Совет Безопасности

Distr.
GENERAL

S/22455
5 April 1991
RUSSIAN
ORIGINAL: ENGLISH

ЗАПИСКА ПРЕДСЕДАТЕЛЯ СОВЕТА БЕЗОПАСНОСТИ

На имя Председателя Совета Безопасности поступило прилагаемое письмо Постоянного наблюдателя Республики Кореи при Организации Объединенных Наций от 5 апреля 1991 года. В соответствии с содержащейся в нем просьбой настоящее письмо распространяется в качестве документа Совета Безопасности.

91-11149 (R6N)619

/...

0142

<u>Приложение</u>

<u>Письмо Постоянного наблюдателя Республики Кореи при Организации
Объединенных Наций от 5 апреля 1991 года на имя Председателя
Совета Безопасности</u>

По поручению моего правительства имею честь препроводить Вам меморандум
правительства Республики Кореи, касающийся ее вступления в члены Организации
Объединенных Наций.

Буду признателен Вам за распространение настоящего письма и прилагаемого к
нему меморандума в качестве документа Совета Безопасности.

Чанг Хи РО
Посол

/...

0143

Добавление

Меморандум правительства Республики Кореи

Правительство Республики Кореи ранее недвусмысленно заявляло о своей позиции относительно членства Республики Кореи в Организации Объединенных Наций, особенно о своей решимости добиваться вступления в члены Организации Объединенных Наций в течение этого года.

Республика Корея, будучи миролюбивым государством, которое стремится и в состоянии выполнять все обязательства, содержащиеся в Уставе Организации Объединенных Наций, отвечает всем требованиям, необходимым для вступления в члены Организации Объединенных Наций. Являясь страной, которая поддерживает дипломатические отношения почти со всеми странами мира, и государством, занимающим двенадцатое место в мире в ряду крупнейших торговых держав, Республика Корея готова внести свой должный вклад в деятельность Организации Объединенных Наций в качестве полноправного члена и в соответствии со своим положением в международном сообществе.

Принцип универсальности, на который опирается Организация Объединенных Наций, предполагает как необходимое условие вступление в члены Организации Объединенных Наций всех суверенных государств, которые выражают такое желание и имеют на это право. Этот принцип как никогда приобретает особую актуальность, поскольку Организация Объединенных Наций играет все более важную роль в эпоху после окончания "холодной войны". Беспрецедентные изменения, происходящие на международной политической арене, отражающие новый дух примирения и сотрудничества, обусловливают необходимость окончательного решения вопроса о вступлении Кореи в Организацию Объединенных Наций.

Как справедливо отмечалось в прошлом году в ходе общих прений на сорок пятой сессии Генеральной Ассамблеи, международное сообщество осознало, что Республика Корея должна без дальнейших промедлений вступить в члены Организации Объединенных Наций.

Стремясь стать членом Организации Объединенных Наций, Республика Корея вновь выражает искреннюю надежду на то, что Корейская Народно-Демократическая Республика (КНДР) также вступит в Организацию Объединенных Наций либо одновременно с Южной Кореей, либо в тот момент, когда Северная Корея сочтет это необходимым. Республика Корея подтверждает свою позицию, заключающуюся в том, что она будет приветствовать вступление КНДР в члены Организации Объединенных Наций.

Кроме того, Республика Корея придерживается той точки зрения, что параллельное членство двух корейских государств в Организации Объединенных Наций никоим образом не наносит ущерба конечной цели объединения Кореи. Параллельное членство должно представлять собой действенную меру укрепления доверия, поскольку оно будет означать твердую приверженность двух корейских государств положениям и принципам Устава Организации Объединенных Наций.

/...

0144

Объединение Восточной и Западной Германии, а также Северного и Южного Йемена в условиях, когда каждое государство сохраняло раздельное членство в Организации Объединенных Наций, подтверждает эту точку зрения и лишает смысла утверждение о том, что членство в Организации Объединенных Наций может увековечить или узаконить разделение корейской нации, препятствуя тем самым усилиям, направленным на объединение Кореи.

Реальность такова, что международное сообщество в течение долгого времени признавало существование Южной и Северной Кореи на Корейском полуострове. Действительно, Корейская Республика и КНДР поддерживают дипломатические отношения со 148 и 105 странами, соответственно. Из этого числа 90 стран поддерживают одновременно дипломатические отношения с обоими корейскими государствами. Каждое корейское государство также отдельно представлено в большинстве межправительственных организаций, включая специализированные учреждения Организации Объединенных Наций. Таким образом, членство Кореи в Организации Объединенных Наций - раздельное или параллельное - станет логическим следствием международной политической реальности.

Будучи искренне убеждена в том, что членство в Организации Объединенных Наций будет содействовать процессу примирения в Корее и ее объединения, а также укреплению мира и безопасности на Корейском полуострове, Республика Корея в духе доброй воли предпринимала все возможные усилия с целью вступления в члены Организации Объединенных Наций одновременно с КНДР в прошлом году, однако эти усилия не увенчались успехом.

Однако, несмотря на эти усилия, КНДР придерживается формулы "единая делегация - одно место", которая не только является непригодной, но и противоречит положениям Устава Организации Объединенных Наций и практике, применяемой Организацией Объединенных Наций и ее специализированными учреждениями. Отсутствие поддержки этой формулы со стороны государств - членов Организации Объединенных Наций в ходе общих прений в прошлом году свидетельствует об их несогласии с формулой Северной Кореи.

Правительство Республики Кореи по-прежнему надеется на вступление двух корейских государств в члены Организации Объединенных Наций в течение этого года. Однако, если КНДР будет и впредь выступать против такого возможного варианта и по каким бы то ни было причинам предпочтет не вступать в члены Организации Объединенных Наций, Республика Корея в порядке осуществления своего суверенного права предпримет необходимые шаги, направленные на ее вступление в Организацию Объединенных Наций до открытия сорок шестой сессии Генеральной Ассамблеи.

Правительство Республики Кореи убеждено в том, что при подавляющей поддержке ее законного стремления вступить в члены Организации Объединенных Наций со стороны государств - членов Организации Республика Корея сможет занять принадлежащее ей по праву место в Организации Объединенных Наций в течение предстоящих месяцев.

0145

S

الأمم المتحدة

مجلس الأمـن

Distr.
GENERAL

S/22455
5 April 1991
ARABIC
ORIGINAL : ENGLISH

<u>مذكرة من رئيس مجلس الامن</u>

وجه المراقب الدائم عن جمهورية كوريا لدى الامم المتحدة إلى رئيس مجلس الامن الرسالة المرفقة المؤرخة ٥ نيسان/ابريل ١٩٩١ . ووفقا للطلب الوارد فيها تعمم هـذه الرسالة بوصفها وثيقة من وثائق مجلس الامن .

0146

(٩١)ن٠٥٧٧   91-11145

.../...

مرفق

رسالة مؤرخة فـي ٥ نيسان/ابريل ١٩٩١
موجهة إلى رئيس مجلس الامن مـن المراقب
الدائم عن جمهورية كوريا لدى الامم المتحدة

بناءً على تعليمات من حكومتي أتشرف بأن أحيل إليكم طيه مذكرة من حكومـة
جمهورية كوريا بشأن انضمامها الى عضوية الامم المتحدة .

وأغدو ممتناً لو تفضلتم بتعميم نص هذه الرسالة والمذكرة المرفقة بهـا ،
بوصفهما وثيقة من وثائق مجلس الامن .

(توقيع) شانغ هي رو
السفير

../..

(٩١)ج.٥٧٧
0147

-٢-

ضميمة

مذكرة من حكومة جمهورية كوريا

أوضحت حكومة جمهورية كوريا في مناسبات سابقة موقفها بشأن انضمام جمهورية
كوريا إلى عضوية الأمم المتحدة لاسيما عزمها على أن تسعى إلى الانضمام إلى عضوية
الأمم المتحدة في خلال هذه السنة .

وجمهورية كوريا بوصفها دولة محبة للسلم وراغبة وقادرة على تنفيذ جميع
الالتزامات الواردة في ميثاق الأمم المتحدة مؤهلة تماما لعضوية الأمم المتحدة .
وبوصفها بلدا له علاقات دبلوماسية عالمية تقريبا ، وبوصفها الدولة الثانية عشرة في
العالم من حيث حجم تجارتها فإنها على استعداد للإسهام على النحو المناسب في أعمال
الأمم المتحدة بوصفها عضوا كامل العضوية وبصورة تتناسب مع مركزها في المجتمع
الدولي .

ويقضي مبدأ العالمية ، الذي تحرص عليه الأمم المتحدة ، بقبول انضمام جميع
من يرغب في الانضمام إلى الأمم المتحدة من الدول ذات السيادة والأهلية للعضوية .
ويكتسب هذا المبدأ أهمية أكبر عن ذي قبل مع قيام الأمم المتحدة بدور متزايد الأهمية
في عصر ما بعد الحرب الباردة . وإن ما يجري في الساحة السياسية الدولية من تغيرات
لم يسبق لها مثيل وتنطوي على روح تصالح وتعاون جديدة يدعو إلى حل مسألة عضوية
كوريا التي طال أمدها .

وكما بُيّن ببلاغة في السنة الماضية في خلال المناقشة العامة في الدورة
الخامسة والأربعين للجمعية العامة أصبح المجتمع الدولي يشعر بأنه ينبغي قبول
انضمام جمهورية كوريا إلى عضوية الأمم المتحدة دون مزيد من الإبطاء .

وإن جمهورية كوريا في سعيها إلى الانضمام إلى عضوية الأمم المتحدة تكرر
الإعراب عن أملها الكبير في أن تنضم جمهورية كوريا الديمقراطية الشعبية أيضا إلى
عضوية الأمم المتحدة إما في نفس الوقت مع الجنوب أو في الوقت الذي يراه الشمال
مناسبا . وتعيد جمهورية كوريا الإعراب عن موقفها المتمثل في ترحيبها بانضمام
جمهورية كوريا الديمقراطية الشعبية إلى عضوية الأمم المتحدة .

../..

٥٠٧٧ن(٩١)

0148

علاوة على ذلك ترى جمهورية كوريا أن العضوية المتوازية لكل من جمهوريتـي كوريا في الأمم المتحدة ليس فيه أي مساس بالغاية النهائيـــة المتمثلـــة في توحيـــد كوريا . فينبغي أن تعتبر العضوية المتوازية إجراءً قويا لبناء الثقة بقدر ما تمثــل الـتزاما راسخا من جانب كلتا جمهوريتي كوريا بأحكام ميثاق الأمم المتحدة ومبادئه .

إن توحيد ألمانيا الشرقية وألمانيا الغربيـــة واليمن الشماليـة واليمـــن الجنوبية ، التي كان لكل منها عضوية مستقلة في الأمم المتحدة يبرر هذا الرأي ويدحـض ما يُزعم من أن عضوية الأمم المتحدة قد تديم الانقسام القومي لكوريا أو تضفي عليـــه الشرعية ، الأمر الذي من شأنه أن يعرقل الجهود الرامية إلى توحيد كوريا .

والواقع هو أن المجتمع الدولي قد اعترف منذ أمد طويل بوجود كوريا الشماليـة وكوريا الجنوبية في شبه الجزيرة الكورية . ولجمهوريـــة كوريا وجمهوريـــة كوريا الديمقراطية الشعبية علاقات دبلوماسيـــة بـ ١٤٨ بلدا و ١٠٥ بلدان ، على التوالـــي . ولتسعين بلدا من هذه البلدان علاقات دبلوماسيـــة مع كل من البلـــدين . ولكل مـــن جمهوريتي كوريا عضوية مستقلة في معظم المنظمات الحكومية الدولية ، بما في ذلـك الوكالات المتخصصة التابعة للأمم المتحدة . وعلى هذا النحو فإن عضوية كوريا في الأمم المتحدة سواءً كانت مستقلة أو متزامنة ستكون أمرا منطقيا ملازما للواقع السياسـي الدولي .

ولقد بذلت جمهورية كوريا كل ما في وسعها وبحسن نية للانضمام إلى عضوية الأمم المتحدة مع جمهورية كوريا الديمقراطية الشعبية في خلال هذه السنة برغبة مخلصة فـي أن تسهم العضوية في الأمم المتحدة في عملية تصالح كوريا وتوحيدها وتعزز أيضا السلم والأمن في شبه الجزيرة الكورية ، لكنها لم تنجح في ذلك .

وعلى الرغم من هذه الجهود تمسكت جمهورية كوريا الديمقراطية الشعبية بصيغة "العضوية الواحدة" وهي ليست غير عملية فحسب وإنما تتعارض أيضا مع أحكام ميثـــاق الأمم المتحدة وممارسات الأمم المتحدة ووكالاتها المتخصصة . وإن عدم تأييد الـدول الأعضاء في الأمم المتحدة لهذه الصيغة في خلال المناقشة العامة في العام الماضي يعبر عن عدم موافقتها على صيغة كوريا الشمالية .

إن حكومة جمهورية كوريا ما زالت تأمل في انضمام كل من جمهوريتي كوريا إلـى العضوية في خلال هذه السنة . بيد أنه إذا ظلت جمهورية كوريا الديمقراطيـة الشعبيـة

ت.٥٧٧(٩١)

0149

على معارضتها لهذا الخيار ، واختارت لأي سبب من الاسباب الا تنضم إلى الامم المتحدة ، فإن جمهورية كوريا ، ممارسة منها لحقها السيادي ، ستتخذ الخطوة اللازمة للانضمام إلى العضوية قبل افتتاح الدورة السادسة والاربعين للجمعية العامة .

وإن حكومة جمهورية كوريا على اقتناع بأن جمهورية كوريا بالتأييد الساحق من جانب الدول الاعضاء في الامم المتحدة لقضية عضويتها المشروعة ستتمكن في الاشهر القادمة من أن تحتل مكانها الشرعي في الامم المتحدة .

- - - - -

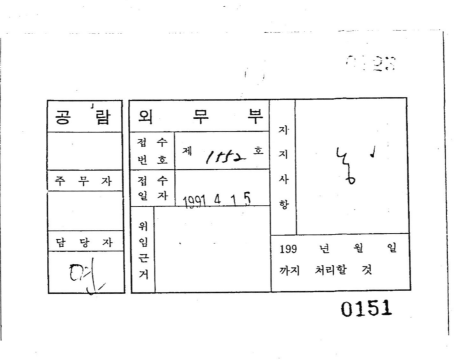

공 람	외 무 부		자 지 사 항	
	접수번호	제 /ff2 호		4
주 무 자	접수일자	1991 4 1 5		
담 당 자	위임근거		199 년 월 일	
			까지 처리할 것	

0151

배　부　처

기 획 실		미 주 국		국제 경제국		외 연 원	
의 전 실		구 주 국		통 상 국		총 무 과	
특 전 실		중 아 국		정 문 국		감사관실	
아 주 국		국제기구 조약국	✓	영 교 국		여 권 과	

0152

ROYAL NORWEGIAN EMBASSY

No. 20/91

The Royal Norwegian Embassy presents its compliments to the Ministry of Foreign Affairs and may herely acknowledge receipt of the Ministry's note No. OGO 91-233 of 8th April, regarding the question of membership to the United Nations of the Republic of Korea.

The Embassy would like to confirm that the content of the note and its enclosure has been made known to the Norwegian authorities.

The Royal Norwegian Embassy avails itself of this opportunity to renew to the Ministry of Foreign Affairs the assurances of its highest consideration.

Seoul, 12 April 1991

To the Ministry of Foreign Affairs
    Seoul

0153

공 람	외 무 부			자 지 사 항	ᄱ
	접 번 수 호	제 /ᄀᄉ/ 호			
주 무 자	접 수 일 자	1991. 4. 1 5			
담 당 자 약	위 임 근 거			199 년 월 일 까지 처리할 것	

0154

배 부 처

기 획 실	미 주 국	국 제 경 제 국	외 연 원
의 전 실	구 주 국	통 상 국	총 무 과
특 전 실	중 아 국	정 문 국	감 사 관 실
아 주 국	국제기구 조 약 국 ✓	영 교 국	여 권 과

0155

AMBASSADE DU GABON
SEOUL

KUNCHANG BLDG. RM.202
238-5. NONHYUN-DONG
KANGNAM-KU

No. ....00194/AGS/CMD...

            L'Ambassade de la République Gabonaise présente
ses compliments au Ministère des Affaires Etrangères de la
République de Corée et a l'honneur d'accuser réception de
sa note No.OGO 91-233 du 8 Avril 1991 par lequel le Gouvernement coréen sollicite le soutien du Gouvernement gabonais
pour l'admission de la République de Corée en tant que membre des Nations Unies, avant l'ouverture de la 46e session
de l'Assemblée Générale des Nations Unies.

            L'Ambassade assure le Ministère des Affaires
Etrangères de la République de Corée que le Gouvernement
gabonais immédiatement saisi donnera la suite escomptée.

            L'Ambassade de la République Gabonaise saisit
cette occasion pour renouveler au Ministère des Affaires
Etrangères de la République de Corée les assurances de sa
très haute considération.

                                    Séoul, le 11 Avril 1991

Ministère des Affaires Etrangères
     de la République de Corée
            (O G O)
            Séoul
            ‾‾‾‾‾

                                                            0156

<번역문>

No. 00194 /AGS/CHD

대한민국 외무부 (OGO) 貴中

　　주한가봉대사관에서　대한민국 외무부에　인사 말씀

올리오며,　한국 정부에서　가봉 정부에　제 46차　U.N. 정기 총회

개최 이전에　대한민국의　U.N. 가입을 위한　지지를　요청 하는

지난 1991年　4月 8日字　공문　No. OGO 91 - 233 에　대하여

회신 드립니다.

　　上記 내용에　대하여　즉각　보고 받은　가봉 정부로

부터　기대할 만한　결과가　주어지리라　확신 드립니다.

　　주한 가봉대사관에서　대한민국 외무부에　쓰가

경의를　표하옵니다.

1991. 4. 11.

가봉대사관.

0157

외 무 부

종 별 : 지 급

번 호 : UNW-0936   일 시 : 91 0416 1930

수 신 : 장관(국연,미중,기정)

발 신 : 주유엔대사

제 목 : 유엔 가입문제(코스타리카)

　　　코스타리카 대표부는 표제관련 아국 메모랜덤을 지지하는 자국 정부 성명 내용을 91.4.15자 안보리문서(S/22495) 로 배포한바, 동 문서를 별첨 송부함.

　　　첨부:상기 안보리문서: UNW(F)-170.끝

　　　(대사 노창희-국장)

국기국   1차보   미주국   안기부

PAGE 1   91.04.17   08:40 DQ

Security Council

Distr.
GENERAL

S/22495
15 April 1991
ENGLISH
ORIGINAL: SPANISH

LETTER DATED 15 APRIL 1991 FROM THE PERMANENT REPRESENTATIVE
OF COSTA RICA TO THE UNITED NATIONS ADDRESSED TO THE
PRESIDENT OF THE SECURITY COUNCIL

On instructions from my Government, I have the honour to transmit to you the following communiqué of the Government of Costa Rica concerning the application by the Republic of Korea to become a member of the United Nations:

"The Government of the Republic of Costa Rica views very sympathetically the desire of the Republic of Korea to become a full member of the United Nations during the course of this year. Such action would be an effective contribution to the principle of universality of international relations and recognition of the sovereignty of States.

"The Government of the Republic of Costa Rica supports the memorandum which the Republic of Korea circulated on 5 April 1991 (S/22455) informing the international community of its wishes."

I should be grateful if you would have the text of this letter circulated as a document of the Security Council.

(Signed) Cristian TATTENBACH
Ambassador
Permanent Representative

91-12065 2271f (E)

#UNW-0936 첨부목

0159

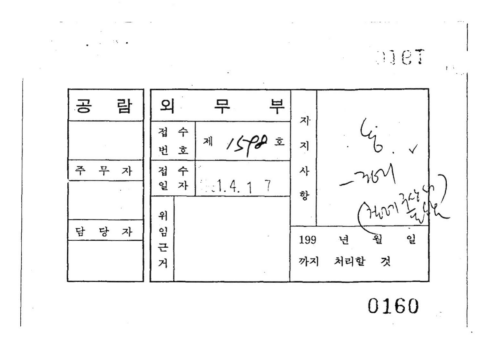

공 람	외 무 부		자 지 사 항	남 ✓ —그에 (제외곤상함)
	접수번호	제 15?? 호		
주 무 자	접수일자	?1. 4. 1 7		
	위임근거		199 년 월 일	
담 당 자			까지 처리할 것	

0160

배   부   처

기 획 실		미 주 국		국제 경제국		외 연 원	
의 전 실		구 주 국		통 상 국		총 무 과	
특 전 실		중 아 국		정 문 국		감사관실	
아 주 국		국제기구 조약국	✓	영 교 국		여 권 과	

0161

EMBASSY OF THE REPUBLIC OF HUNGARY
SEOUL

Seoul, April 17, 1991

No. 65-2/1991

        The Embassy of the Republic of Hungary presents its compliments
to the Ministry of Foreign Affairs of the Republic of Korea and has the
honour – with reference to the latter's Note No. OGO 91-233 – to communicate that in accordance with its previously clarified position the
Government of the Republic of Hungary supports the efforts made by the
Government of the Republic of Korea aimed at occupying its seat in the
United Nations' Organisation as soon as possible.

        The Embassy of the Republic of Hungary avails itself of this
opportunity to renew to the Ministry of Foreign Affairs of the Republic
of Korea the assurances of its highest consideration.

Ministry of Foreign Affairs
of the Republic of Korea
S e o u l

14415

기 안 용 지

분류기호 문서번호	국연 2031-	기 안 용 지 (전화:)	시 행 상 특별취급	
보존기간	영구·준영구. 10.5.3.1.	장	관	
수 신 처 보존기간				
시행일자	1991. 4. 18.	↳		

보 조 기 관	국 장	전 결	협 조 기 관		문 서 통 제	
	과 장	₩.			1991. 4. 19	
기안책임자		송 영 완			발 송 인	
경 유 수 신 참 조		EM 공관장	발 신 명 의		1991.4.19	
제 목		아국의 유연가입문제에 관한 안보리문서 배포				

연 : EM-0009 (91.4.6)

연호, 유연가입에 관한 아국 정부각서가 91.4.5.자 안보리

문서로 91.4.8. 배포된 바, 동 문서사본 및 유연가입에 관한 절차

요약을 별첨 송부하니 업무에 참고하시기 바랍니다.

첨 부 : 1. 안보리문서(S/22455) 1부.

2. 유연가입 절차요약 1부. 끝.

0163

1505-25(2-1) 일(1)갑
85. 9. 9. 승인 "내가아낀 종이 한장 늘어나는 나라살림"

190mm×268mm 인쇄용지 2급 60g/㎡
가 40-41 1989. 6. 8

안보리문서 배포 (언어권별)

(104개 공관)

1. 영   어 : 주 일본, 필리핀, 미얀마, 네팔, 말련, 인니, 뉴질랜드, PNG,
   (59)
   브르네이, 호주, 싱가폴, 인도, 스리랑카, 파키스탄, 몽골,

   태국, 방글라데시, 휘지, 미국, 카나다, 브라질, 영국,

   아일랜드, 노르웨이, 핀랜드, 제네바, 스위스, 터키, 유네스코,

   ~~유네스코~~, 네덜란드, 이태리, 교황청, 불가리아, 독일, 오지리,

   유고, 헝가리, 스웨덴, 덴마크, EC, 희랍, 폴투갈, 폴랜드,

   루마니아, 체코, 나이제리아, 가나, 이란, 말라위, 나미비아,

   시에라레온, 모리셔스, 케냐, 레바논, 이디오피아, 우간다,

   스와질랜드, 잠비아 대사, 주홍콩 총영사

2. 불   어 : 주 아이티, 프랑스, 벨기에, 코트디브와르, 가봉, 자이르,
   (12)
   알제리, 튀니지, 모로코, 모리타니아, 카메룬, 세네갈 대사

3. 서반아어 : 주 멕시코, 도미니카, 자메이카, 과테말라, T&T, 페루,
   (19)
   엘살바돌, 코스타리카, 파나마, 수리남, 에쿠아돌, 볼리비아,

   파라과이, 콜롬비아, 베네주엘라, 칠레, 알젠틴, 우루과이,

   스페인 대사

4. 아 랍 어 : 바레인, 카탈, 아랍에미리트, 사우디, 리비아, 수단, 오만,
   (11)
   예멘, 요르단 대사, 주카이로 총영사

5. 중 국 어 : 주 중국, 북경 대사
   (2)

6. 노   어 : ~~주~~ 소련대사
   (1)

유엔가입절차 요약

91. 4. 16.
국제연합과

1. 가입신청방식

○ 아국 유엔가입문제는 최초로 유엔가입을 신청한 49.1.19. 이래 안보리에
계류중임. 따라서 아국은 ⅰ) 유엔사무총장에게 유엔가입문제 재심청구서
제출, ⅱ) 유엔사무총장에게 가입신청서 재제출, ⅲ) 우방국에 의한 아국
가입문제 재심 결의안 안보리 제출방식중 한가지를 택하여 유엔가입을
신청할 수 있음. (북한의 유엔가입문제도 49.2.9. 이래 안보리에 계류중)

참고   안보리는 특정안건에 대한 심의를 완료했다고 결정하지 않는한
계속 계류중인 것으로 간주함. (현재까지 안보리가 심의완료를
선언한 경우는 거의 없음)

2. 신청시기

○ 유엔안보리 의사규칙 제59조에 의하면, 신규회원가입은 정기총회 개시
35일전까지 안보리 가입심사위원회가 가입 신청을 심사, 안보리에 보고
하도록 규정하고 있음.

○ 또한 제60조에 의하면 안보리는 가입신청에 대한 권고를 정기 총회개시
25일전에 총회에 제출해야 하나 특별한 경우(in special circumstances)
에는 상기 60조의 적용을 배제(Waiver)할 수 있다는 예외조항을 포함하고
있음.

0165

안보리 가입심사위원회(Committee on the Admission of New Members)는
안보리 이사국(15개국) 전체로 구성되며, 안보리의 가입신청심의에 앞서
가입신청서(또는 결의안)를 검토하여 동 결과를 안보리에 보고함.

3. 가입신청 시한 문제

○ 안보리 의사규칙 60조의 예외조항은 1975-84년 기간중 10개국의 가입신청
  심의시 이미 원용된 바 있음. 즉, 안보리의 권고결의안의 총회 회부시한
  적용이 배제됨.

○ 특히 제45차 총회(1990)부터는 총회 회기가 정기총회기간(통상 9-12월)과는
  무관하게 차기총회 개막직전까지 계속되는 것으로 간주됨에 따라 안보리 의사
  규칙 60조의 적용에 따른 시한상의 제약은 상대적으로 감소됨.

○ 단, 가입신청시한문제가 안보리에서 강력히 제기될 경우 60조 적용여부
  자체를 표결에 부치게 될 것인바, 이 경우는 절차문제로 간주되어 단순
  9개국 찬성으로 결정됨. (거부권 불인정)

4. 가입신청의 안보리의제 채택

○ 안보리의장은 가입신청서 또는 우방국의 가입문제 관련 결의안을 접수하면
  안보리에 회부하여, 동 문제를 안보리 의제로 채택할지 여부를 consensus
  또는 표결로 채택함. (표결시 단순 9개국 찬성으로 의제 채택 결정)

○ 안보리의제 채택시 안보리의장은 안보리 가입심사위원회에 동 가입 문제를
  심의토록 회부함.

5. 안보리 가입심사위원회 심의

○ 가입심사위원회에서는 가입신청의 안보리 회부여부를 콘센서스로 채택함이
  일반적이나, 반대국이 있을 경우, 단순 9개국 찬성으로 안보리 회부를
  결정함. (거부권 불인정)

0166

6. 안보리 가입권고 결의 채택

○ 안보리는 가입신청국이 평화애호국이며 헌장상 의무를 수행할 능력과
의사가 있는가 여부를 판단하고, 가입권고 여부를 상임이사국 5개국을
포함한 9개국 찬성으로 결의하여 총회개시 25일전에 안보리 토의기록
(권고하지 않을 경우에는 특별보고서)과 함께 총회에 송부함. (거부권 인정)

7. 총회의 안보리 권고안 심의 및 가입결의안 채택

○ 안보리의 권고에 따라 총회는 가입신청국이 평화애호국이고 헌장상
의무를 이행할 능력과 의사가 있는지 여부를 검토하고, 가입신청국의
유엔가입에 관한 총회결의안에 대해 표결, 투표결과 총투표국의 2/3
다수 획득시 가입 확정

8. 안보리 및 총회 표결관련 참고사항

○ 안보리 및 총회에서의 표결시에는 참석하여 투표한 국가(present and
voting states)의 투표를 기준으로 하는 바, 불참국, 기권국은 투표국
으로 간주치 않음. (안보리 상임이사국의 경우도 불참 또는 기권시
Veto 행사로서 인정되지 않음)

0167

보 도 자 료

외 무 부

제   호   문의전화 : 720-2408~10   보도일시 : . . . . : 시

제 목 : 유엔가입문제에 관한 각서 (2)

(상단 우측 손글씨: 추후 더많은나라가 있음 반영할때까지 hold)

가. 유엔가입문제에 관한 우리의 입장을 밝힌 정부각서(91.4.5자)가 유엔안보리
　　 문서로 배포되자, 우리의 유엔가입을 지지하는 국제여론이 확산되고 있다.

나. 특히 코스타리카 정부는 아국의 유엔가입에 대한 입장을 지지하는 성명을
　　 91.4.15자 유엔 안보리문서로 배포하였다. 코스타리카 정부는 성명에서
　　 "유엔에 가입코자 하는 한국정부의 입장을 환영하며 이는 유엔의 보편성
　　 원칙과 각국의 주권존중원칙을 강화하는 조치로서 이를 지지한다"고 밝혔다.

다. 또한, 볼리비아의 주요일간지 "호이"(Hoy)지는 4.15자 우리의 유엔가입에
　　 관한 사설기사에서 아국 정부각서 내용을 상세히 전재한 후, 현재 안보리의
　　 5개 상임이사국중 중국이 거부권을 행사할 수 있으나 그 가능성은 희박하며
　　 만약 거부권사용시 전세계국가와 중국간에 냉전의 앙금이 남게될 것"이라고
　　 평하고 우리의 유엔가입을 전폭적으로 지지함을 밝혔다.

라. 뿐만 아니라, 미국 아틀란타시의 "아틀란타 콘스티튜션"(Atlanta Constitution)
　　 지는 유엔가입에 관한 아국의 입장을 지지하고 남북한의 유엔가입이 한반도의
　　 평화와 안전에 기여함은 물론 통일을 지향하는 잠정조치로서 국제사회의 지지를
　　 받고있음을 보도했다.

마. 예멘의 최대일간지인 "알타라"(Al-Thawra)지도 4면 톱기사로 아국문제를 다루면서
　　 유엔가입에 관한 우리의 입장을 소상히 보도했다.   끝.

양	담 당	과 장	극 장
고 재			

0168

주 과 테 말 라 대 사 관

과정 20311- 146

1991. 4. 19.

수신 장 관

참조 국제기구조약국장, 미주국장.

제목 유엔 가입.

대: EM-8

연: GUW-125

연호 온두라스 외무성의 아국 유엔 가입에 대한 지지 공한을 별첨
송부합니다.

별첨: 동 공한 사본 1부.   끝.

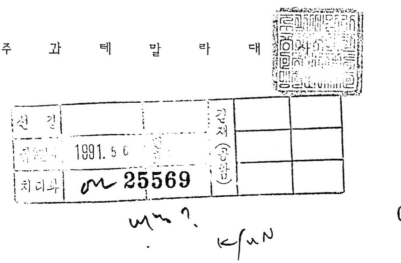

주 과 테 말 라 대

0169

SECRETARIA DE RELACIONES EXTERIORES
DE LA
REPUBLICA DE HONDURAS

No. 017-DA.

La Secretaría de Relaciones Exteriores saluda atentamente a la Honorable Embajada de la República de Corea y tiene el honor de acusar recibo de su nota No. KGU/114/91 del 12 de este mes, con la que acompaña el memorandum referente a la admisión de la República de Corea como Estado Miembro de las Naciones Unidas.

El Gobierno de Honduras tradicionalmente ha apoyado la justa y legítima aspiración de la República de Corea en este sentido. En consecuencia, la Secretaría de Relaciones Exteriores se complace en manifestar que de inmediato se girarán las instrucciones pertinentes al Representante Permanente en las Naciones Unidas para que, llegado el momento, apoye sin reservas la admisión de la República de Corea como miembro de la Organización.

La Secretaría de Relaciones Exteriores aprovecha esta oportunidad para reiterar a la Honorable Embajada de la República de Corea las seguridades de su más elevada consideración.

Tegucigalpa M.D.C., 18 de abril de 1991

HONORABLE
EMBAJADA DE LA REPUBLICA DE COREA
GUATEMALA.

0170

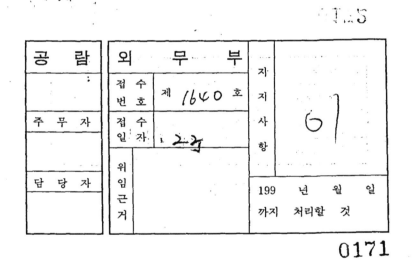

공 람	외　무　부	지지사항	61
：	접수번호	제 1640 호	
주　무　자	접수일자	22	
담　당　자	위임근거		199　년　월　일 까지　처리할　것

0171

배 부 처

기 획 실		미 주 국		국제 경제국		외 연 원	
의 전 실		구 주 국		통 상 국		총 무 과	
특 전 실		중 아 국		정 문 국	·	감사관실	
아 주 국		국제기구 조 약 국	✓	영 교 국		여 권 과	

0172

AUSTRIAN EMBASSY

Ref.No. 75-RES/91

The Austrian Embassy presents its compliments to
the Ministry of Foreign Affairs of the Republic of Korea and has
the honour to acknowledge receipt of its verbal note No. OGO - 233
dated 8 April 1991, the contents of which have been brought to the
attention of the Austrian authorities.

The Austrian Embassy avails itself of this opportunity to renew to the Ministry of Foreign Affairs of the Republic
of Korea the assurances of its highest consideration.

Seoul, 17 April 1991

THE MINISTRY OF FOREIGN AFFAIRS
OF THE REPUBLIC OF KOREA
S E O U L

0173

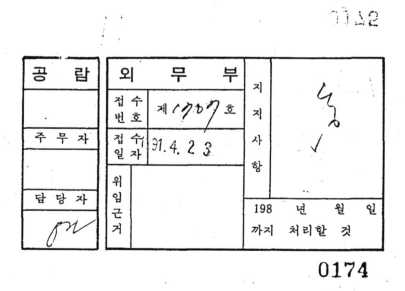

공 람	외 무 부		지지사항	낭 ✓
	접수번호	제 1127 호		
주 무 자	접수일자	91.4. 2 3		
	위임근거		198 년 월 일	
담 당 자			까지 처리할 것	

0174

배　부　처

기획실	미주국	국제 경제국	외 연 원	
의전실	구주국	통상국	총무과	
특전실	중아국	정문국	감사관실	
아주국	국제기구 조약국	영교국	여권과	

0175

AMBASSADE D'HAITI, SEOUL

19/91

The Embassy of the Republic of Haiti presents its compliments to the Ministry of Foreign Affairs and has the honour to acknowledge receipt of the Note OGO 91-233 dated 8 April 1991, the contents of which have been duly noted.

This Embassy informs to the Ministry of Foreign Affairs that the above important communication has been transmitted to the Ministry of Foreign Affairs of the Republic of Haiti .

The Embassy of the Republic of Haiti avails itself of this opportunity to renew to the Ministry of Foreign Affairs the assurances of its highest consideration

SEOUL, 22 April 1991

0176

관리
번호 91
-2736

발 신 전 보

번 호 : EM-0016   910426 1657 ED   종별 : ____

수 신 : 주 EM 공관장 대사. ♣♣♣♣

발 신 : 장 관   (국연)

제 목 : 유엔가입추진 (각국반응)

연 : EM-0009

연호 정부각서의 안보리문서 배포이후 4.25.까지의 각국 주요
반응을 통보하니 참고바람.

1. 코스타리카

　ㅇ 아국의 유엔가입 입장을 지지하는 "코"정부의 성명을
　　91.4.15자 유엔 안보리문서로 배포

　　- 동 성명내용 ; 유엔에 가입코자 하는 한국정부의
　　　입장을 환영하며 이는 유엔의 보편성원칙과 각국의
　　　주권존중의 원칙을 강화하는 조치로서 이를 지지함.

2. 미 국

　ㅇ 미국무부 보도지침(4.22자)을 통하여 부쉬 미대통령이
　　제45차 유엔총회 기조연설에서 유엔의 보편성원칙에 따른
　　아국의 유엔가입지지 발언을 하였음을 강조하고, 한국의
　　유엔가입이 한반도 통일에 기여할 것이라고 밝힘.

/계속...

제1차버전 :

		기안자 성명		과 장		국 장		차 관	장 관	
앙고 재	91년 4월 26일 N과	송영완								외신과통제

보 안 통 제

0177

3. 헝가리, 온두라스, 가봉, 태국、칠레

    ○ 아국의 유엔가입을 지지한다는 내용의 구상서를 송부해옴. 끝

4. 기   타 (각국언론에서 아국의 유엔가입지지 사설, 기사 게재)

    - 예멘의 최대일간지 "Al-Thawar" (4.2)

    - 미국 아틀란타시 일간지 "Atlanta Constitution" (4.13)

    - 볼리비아 주요일간지 "Hoy" (4.15)

    - 카나다 일간지 "La Presse" (4.17)

    - 우간다 일간지 "The Star" 및 "NGABO" (4.19-20).   끝.

91. 12. 31. 입력

(국제기구조약국장 대리)

검토필(1991. 6. 30)

0178

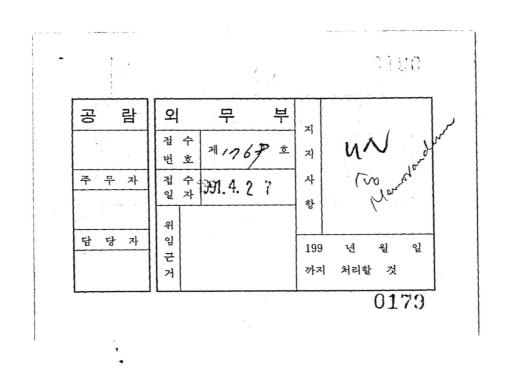

공 람	외 무 부		지지사항	UN Two Memorandum
	접수번호	제 *1767* 호		
주 무 자	접수일자	1991.4.2 7		
	위임근거		199 년 월 일 까지 처리할 것	
담 당 자				

0179

배 부 처

기 획 실		미 주 국		국제 경제국		외 연 원	
의 전 실		구 주 국		통 상 국		총 무 과	
특 전 실		중 아 국		정 문 국		감 사 관 실	
아 주 국		국제기구 조 약 국	✓	영 교 국		여 권 과	

0180

Note No. 20/91

The Embassy of Sweden presents its compliments to
the Ministry of Foreign Affairs and has the
honour to acknowledge receipt of its Note No. OGO
91/233 concerning membership of the United
Nations the contents of which has been brought to
the notice of the Swedish Government.

The Embassy of Sweden avails itself of this
opportunity to renew to the Ministry of Foreign
Affiars the assurances of its highest
consideration.

Seoul, 17 April 1991

To the Ministry of Foreign Affairs

SEOUL

0181

Postadress	Gatuadress	Telefon	Telex	Telefax
C.P. O. BOX 3577 SEOUL REPUBLIC OF KOREA	BOYUNG BLDG ,8TH FLOOR 108-2, PYUNG-DONG, CHONGRO-KU, SEOUL	720-4767 738-0846 738-1149	27231 SVENSK	(02)733-1317

신뢰받는 정부되고 받쳐주는 국민되자

주 코 스 타 리 카 대 사 관

코스타(정)20311- 30   1991. 4. 29

수 신 : 장 관

참 조 : 국제기구조약국장, 미주국장

제 목 : 유엔가입 추진 관련 자료 송부

      연 : COW-0174(91.4.19)

      대 : WCO-0079

    코스타리카 정부의 아국 유엔 가입 메모랜덤 지지 안보리 문서 배포와 관련, 연호 외무성으로부터 입수한 주재국 유엔대사의 외상앞 4.17입자 보고공문 사본을 별첨 송부 합니다.

    첨 부 : 동 보고공문 사본 1부. 끝.

           예고 : 91.12.31입반

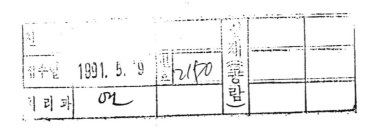

주 코 스 타 리 카 대 사

0182

UNOFFICIAL TRANSLATION

REPUBLIC OF COSTA RICA
MINISTRY OF FOREIGN AFFAIRS
AND RELIGION

DGPE/SGO1/319/91

F.A.C.S.I.M.I.L.

TO: MR. DEOK SO JEONG
        CHARGE D'AFFAIRS A.I.
        EMBASSY OF KOREA
        FAX #55-40-18

FROM: JOSE DE J. CONEJO,
      DIRECTOR GENERAL OF FOREIGN POLICY

DATE: APRIL 18, 1991

REFERENCE: SUPPORT TO REQUEST

No. OF PAGES: 2

FOR YOUR KIND INFORMATION, I HEREBY SEND THE TEXT OF DOCUMENT S/22495
CIRCULATED BY THE SECURITY COUNCIL OF THE UNITED NATIONS
AS REQUESTED BY THE GOVERNMENT OF THE REPUBLIC OF COSTA RICA.

SINCERELY,

cc/ file

0183

UNOFFICIAL TRANSLATION

PERMANENT MISSION OF COSTA RICA
AT THE UNITED NATIONS

FAX COVER

TO: MR. BERND NIEHAUS QUESADA, MINISTER OF FOREIGN AFFAIRS AND
      RELIGION

      ATTN: MR. JOSE DE J. CONEJO, DIRECTOR GENERAL OF FOREIGN POLICY

FROM: AMBASSADOR CRISTIAN TATTENBACH, PERMANENT REPRESENTATIVE
      AT THE UNITED NATIONS

REFERENCE: REQUEST OF ADMISSION OF THE REPUBLIC OF KOREA AS A MEMBER
           OF THE UNITED NATIONS

DATE: APRIL 17, 1991

NUMBER OF PAGES INCLUDING FAX COVER

FAX ACCESS NUMBER: (212) 986-6842

COMMENTS: I HAVE THE HONOUR TO SEND YOU THE DOCUMENT NO. S/22495 OF
APRIL 15 , 1991, TRANSMITTED TO THE PRESIDENT OF THE SECURITY COUNCIL, IN
COMPLIANCE WITH YOUR INSTRUCTIONS CONTAINED IN FAX #DGPE/SGO1/250/91,
RECEIVED ON APRIL 9, 1991, IN WHICH WE SUPPORT THE REQUEST OF ADMISSION OF
THE REPUBLIC OF KOREA, AS A STATE MEMBER OF THE INTERNATIONAL ORGANIZATION.

                                        SINCERELY,

                                        TATTENBACH (signature)

0184

REPUBLICA DE COSTA RICA
MINISTERIO DE RELACIONES EXTERIORES Y CULTO
_____

DGPE/ SGOI/ 319 / 91

F.A.C.S.I.M.I.L.

PARA: Sr. Deok So Jeong,
        Encargado de Negocios a.i.
        Embajada de Corea
        FAX #554018

DE: Sr. José de J. Conejo,
        Director General de Política Exterior

FECHA: 18 de abril de 1991

ASUNTO: Apoyo a Solicitud.

PAGINAS: 2

****

Para su estimable conocimiento, hago remisión del texto del documento S/22495 hecho circular por el Consejo de Seguridad de la Organización de las Naciones Unidas a solicitud del Gobierno de la República de Costa Rica.

Atentamente,

VM/gemr
cc: Archivo

0185

MISION P ANENTE DE COSTA RICA
ANTE LAS NACIONES UNIDAS
811 EAST 43RD ST.
NEW YORK. N. Y. 10017

PORTADA DE FAX

PARA: SR. LIC. DON BERND NIEHAUS QUESADA
MINISTRO DE RELACIONES EXTERIORES Y CULTO

DE: ATT. SR. JOSÉ DE J. CONEJO, DIRECTOR GENERAL
DE POLÍTICA EXTERIOR
EMBAJADOR CRISTIÁN TATTENBACH, REPRESENTANTE
PERMANENTE ANTE LAS NACIONES UNIDAS

ASUNTO: SOLICITUD DE LA REPÚBLICA DE COREA DE INGRESAR
COMO MIEMBRO DE LAS NACIONES UNIDAS

FECHA: ABRIL 17 DE 1991

Número de páginas incluyendo ésta: DOS

FAX ACCESS NUMBER: (212) 986-6842

COMENTARIOS: TENGO EL HONOR DE REMITIRLE EL DOCUMENTO No. S/22495
DEL 15 DE ABRIL DE 1991, TRASMITIDO AL PRESIDENTE DEL CONSEJO DE
SEGURIDAD EN CUMPLIMIENTO DE SUS INSTRUCCIONES CONTENIDAS EN EL
FAX #DGPE/SGOI/250/91 RECIBIDA EL 9 DE ABRIL DE 1991, POR MEDIO DE
LA CUAL APOYAMOS LA SOLICITUD DEL GOBIERNO DE LA REPÚBLICA DE COREA,
PARA INGRESAR COMO ESTADO MIEMBRO DE LA ORGANIZACIÓN MUNDIAL.

ATENTAMENTE,

POR TATTENBACH
CRUN

0186

S

NACIONES
UNIDAS

Consejo de Seguridad

Distr.
GENERAL

S/22495
15 de abril de 1991

ORIGINAL: ESPAÑOL

CARTA DE FECHA 15 DE ABRIL DE 1991 DIRIGIDA AL PRESIDENTE
DEL CONSEJO DE SEGURIDAD POR EL REPRESENTANTE PERMANENTE
DE COSTA RICA ANTE LAS NACIONES UNIDAS

Siguiendo instrucciones de mi Gobierno, tengo el honor de transmitirle el siguiente comunicado del Gobierno de Costa Rica, relacionado con la solicitud de ingreso de la República de Corea, como Miembro de las Naciones Unidas:

"El Gobierno de la República de Costa Rica ve con la mayor simpatía la aspiración de la República de Corea de ingresar como Miembro pleno de la Organización de las Naciones Unidas, en el transcurso del presente año, cuyo acto constituiría un aporte efectivo al principio de la universalidad de las relaciones internacionales y el reconocimiento de la soberanía de los Estados.

El Gobierno de la República de Costa Rica apoya el memorándum de la República de Corea que circuló el día 5 de abril de 1991 (S/22455) mediante el que se expresa a la comunidad internacional el deseo de la República de Corea."

Agradecería a Vuestra Excelencia que tuviera a bien hacer circular el texto de la presente carta como documento del Consejo de Seguridad.

(Firmado) Cristián TATTENBACH
Embajador
Representante Permanente

91-12068 1261i

0187

주 볼 리 비 아 대 사 관

볼비(정) 700 - *101*   1991.   5.   2.

수 신 : 장   관

참 조 : 국제기구조약국장

제 목 : 아국 유엔가입 지지 주재국 외무장관 친서 전달

        연 : BVW - 0143

     연호 Carlos Iturralde 주재국 외무장관의 장관님앞 친서를 별첨 전달합니다.

첨 부 : 상기 친서봉투 1개. 끝.

República de Bolivia

Ministerio de Relaciones Exteriores y Culto

La Paz 8 de abril de 1991
GM ₦ 066

Excelentísimo señor Ministro:

Tengo el alto honor de dirigirme a Vuestra Excelencia con motivo de expresarle mis más sinceras felicitaciones al haber asumido las funciones de Ministro de Relaciones Exteriores de la República de Corea, deseándole el mayor de los éxitos en el ejercicio de las mismas .

Asimismo, deseo manifestarle la profunda satisfacción del Gobierno Constitucional de Bolivia, y del mio propio, por el positivo desarrollo de las relaciones de cooperación económica y técnica entre nuestros países, que conducen al fortalecimiento de los vínculos de amistad de nuestros pueblos. En particular, merece destacarse especialmente la asistencia que otorga su Ilustrado Gobierno para el desarrollo de la sericultura en Bolivia, que se ha hecho tangible a través de la última donación destinada al Instituto de Investigaciones del Departamento de Santa Cruz.

Mas aún, estoy convencido de que la Tercera Reunión de la Comisión Mixta Boliviano ₦ Coreana, prevista para el segundo semestre del presente año, contribuirá decisivamente al fortalecimiento de estos lazos de amistad y cooperación.

Señor Ministro, el gobierno boliviano sigue con particular interés las acciones que viene llevando a cabo su Ilustrado Gobierno para hallar una justa y pronta solución a los problemas que aquejan a la Península Coreana.

Excmo. señor
D. Sang Ock Lee
MINISTRO DE RELACIONES EXTERIORES
DE LA REPUBLICA DE COREA
Seúl ₦ República de Corea

0189

República de Bolivia

Ministerio de Relaciones Exteriores y Culto

Gabinete del Ministro

Bolivia, consecuente con los principios que rigen su política internacional, apoyará toda acción que, partiendo del diálogo y del respeto a las normas del Derecho Internacional, contribuyan a llegar a un arreglo de la mencionada problemática.

En este contexto, vé con simpatía las gestiones de la República de Corea para obtener su ingreso al seno de las Naciones Unidas, con el sincero convencimiento de que ello contribuirá a establecer definitivamente la paz y la seguridad en la península coreana.

El Gobierno boliviano es consciente de la necesidad de fortalecer la paz y la seguridad internacionales, más aún en el mundo actual caracterizado por una mayor interdependencia de las naciones y por un proceso de reestructuración de las relaciones internacionales, por lo que considera urgente el resolver los conflictos que afectan todavía a la Comunidad Internacional. Es por ello que apoyará toda acción que pueda tomar el Ilustrado Gobierno de la República de Corea que, en el contexto de estos principios, promueva la realización de los altos ideales de la unificación del pueblo coreano.

Con este motivo, hago propicia la oportunidad para reiterarle, señor Ministro, las seguridades de mi más alta consideración.

Lic. Carlos Iturralde Ballivián
MINISTRO DE RELACIONES EXTERIORES
Y CULTO

0190

주 멕 시 코 대 사 관

멕 정 700 - *207*   1991. 5. 2.

수 신 : 외무부장관

참 조 : 국제기구조약국장

제 목 : 유엔가입 지지교섭

　　　연 : MXW - 0465

　　　연호 주재국 정부로 부터 접수한 아국 유엔 가입 교섭에 대한

주재국 회신 공문 사본을 별첨 보고합니다.

　　　첨 부 : 관련문서 사본.끝.

주 　 멕 　 시 　 코 　 대 　 사

선 결			결재 (공람)		
접수일시	1991. 5 6	번호			
서리과	遞 25571				

무슨내용이리 7. 0191

La Secretaría de Relaciones Exteriores
saluda muy atentamente a la Embajada de la República de
Corea y tiene el honor de hacer referencia a su atenta -
nota KMX/91/073 de fecha 9 de abril de 1991, con la cual
tuvo a bien enviar a esta Cancillería el memorándum que -
contiene la posición de ese país con respecto a su admisión como miembro de las Naciones Unidas, antes de la -
apertura de la 46a. Sesión de la Asamblea General de la
Organización de las Naciones Unidas.

Sobre el particular, la Secretaría se
permite manifestar que ha tomado debida nota sobre el -
contenido del memorándum mencionado, el cual será objeto
de un examen esmerado.

La Secretaría de Relaciones Exteriores
aprovecha la oportunidad para reiterar a la Embajada de
la República de Corea las seguridades de su más alta y
distinguida consideración.

México, D.F., a 18 de abril de 1991 .

A la Embajada de la
República de Corea
C i u d a d.

0192

주 핀 랜 드 대 사 관

핀 (정) 20730 - ///   1991.   5.   3.

수신 : 장관

참조 : 국제기구조약국장

제목 : 유엔관련 각서 수교

    연 : FNW - 0104

    연호 아국의 유엔관련 각서에 대한 주재국 [정부의 구상서]
사본을 별첨 송부하오니 참고하시기 바랍니다. 끝.

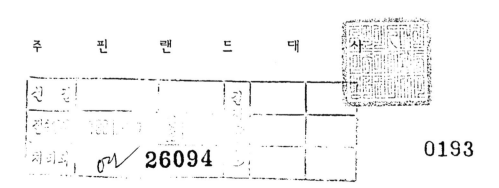

                    0193

MINISTRY FOR FOREIGN AFF=
OF FINLAND

No. 12339

The Ministry for Foreign Affairs of Finland present their compliments to the Embassy of the Republic of Korea and have the honour to acknowledge receipt of the Embassy's note no. KFN-4-23-91 of April 11, 1991, with the Memorandum of the Government of the Republic of Korea concerning its membership in the United Nations, which has been submitted to the Security Council of the United Nations.

The contents of this kind communication have been duly noted.

The Ministry for Foreign Affairs avail themselves of this opportunity to renew to the Embassy of the Republic of Korea the assurance of their highest consideration.

Helsinki, April 22, 1991

To
the Embassy of the
Republic of Korea
H e l s i n k i

0194

AE 02   27/5583L/ads

"신뢰받는 정부되고 밭여주는 국민되자"
주 엘 살 바 돎 대 사 관

주엘정 20700 - 98   1991. 5. 6.
수신   외무부장관
참조   국제기구조약국장, 미주국장
제목   유엔 가입 추진 메모랜덤
        인 : ESW-0079

        주재국 외무성은 91.4.9자 당관 구상서에 대하여 JOSE R. MEJIA 정부
국장 명의로, 아국 정부의 메모랜덤 내용에 유의 및 전통적인 양국 이해에서 아국의
유엔 가입을 지지할 것임을 회보해 왔는바, 동 회람 사본을 별첨 송부합니다.

첨부 : 동 구상서(회람) 1부.   끝.

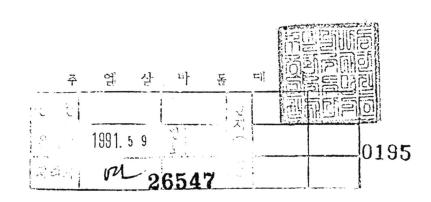

0195

26547

MINISTERIO DE RELACIONES EXTERIORES
REPÚBLICA DE EL SALVADOR, C.A.

SECRETARIA DE ESTADO

DGPE/No. 004579   San Salvador, 23 de abril de 1991

SEÑOR ENCARGADO:

Tengo el agrado de dirigirme a Vuestra Señoría - para avisar recibo de su notificación de 10 de abril del presente año, adjunto a la cual remite copia del memorándum de -- Vuestro Ilustrado Gobierno sobre la Membresía de la República de Corea ante las Naciones Unidas.

Sobre el particular, comunico a usted que ésta - Cancillería ha tomado nota de los conceptos de dicho memorándum, los cuales serán considerados con el interés que siempre ha caracterizado las relaciones entre nuestros dos países.

Aprovecho la oportunidad para reiterar a Vuestra - Señoría las seguridades de mi más alta y distinguida consideración.

JOSE ROBERTO MEJIA TRABANINO
DIRECTOR GENERAL DE POLITICA EXTERIOR A.I.

EXCELENTISIMO SEÑOR
SANG BAIK YOO;
ENCARGADO DE NEGOCIOS A.I.
DE LA REPUBLICA DE COREA,
P R E S E N T E.-

0196

공 람	외 무 부		지 지 사 항	
	접 수 번 호	제 2160 호		
주 무 자	접 수 일 자	1991. 7 7		
담 당 자 (서명)	위 임 근 거		199 년 월 일 까지 처리할 것	

0197

배 부 처

기 획 실		미 주 국		국 제 경 제 국		외 연 원	
의 전 실		구 주 국		통 상 국		총 무 과	
특 전 실		중 아 국		정 문 국		감사관실	
아 주 국		국제기구 조 약 국	✓	영 교 국		여 권 과	

0198

بسم الله الرحمن الرحيم

EMBASSY OF THE UNITED ARAB EMIRATES

S E O U L

سفارة دولة الإمارات العربية المتحدة

سيـــــؤول

Date : 15/5/1991

Ref : 1/4/9 - ١٥٥

التاريخ :

الموافق :

الاشارة :

الصادر :

The Embassy of the United Arab Emirates presents its compliments to the Ministry of the Foreign Affairs of the Republic of Korea and has the honour to refer to your note No. OGO91-233 dated 8th, April, 1991, and inform you that the United Arab Emirates Government will render its support   for   the Republic of Korea for its admission to the United Nation Membership in the 46th Session of the General Assembly of the United Nations.

The Embassy of the United Arab Emirates avails itself of this opportunity to express to the Ministry of Foreign Affairs   the assurances of its highest consideration.

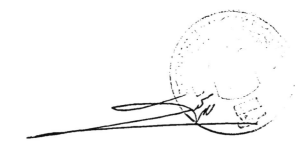

To : The Ministry of Foreign Affairs - S E O U L
                                          Republic of Korea

0199

<table>
<tr><td>관리
번호</td><td>91
-3256</td></tr>
</table>

<table>
<tr><td>분류번호</td><td>보존기간</td></tr>
<tr><td></td><td></td></tr>
</table>

발 신 전 보

WMG-0241   910515 1129 CT

번   호 : _____   종별 : _____

수   신 : 주   수신처 참조   대사. 총영사

발   신 : 장   관   (국연)

제   목 : 유연가입추진

연 : EM-9, 13, 17

아국의 유연가입문제에 관한 91.4.5.자 정부각서를 안보리문서로 회람한 이래 아측입장에 대한 귀재국(~~검압국~~) 반응 상금 미접인 바, ~~주재국(접압국) 외무성을 겹촉, 아국의 유연가입에 대한 지지를 확보하고~~ 접촉결과 지급 보고바람.   끝.

예 고 : 1991.12.31. 일반

(국제기구조약국장   문동석)

수신처 : 몽고, ~~불가리~~ ~~(루셈다 로코)~~, 리비아, 튀니지, 나미비아 대사

검토필(1991.6.30)

<table>
<tr><td>보 안
통 제</td><td></td></tr>
</table>

<table>
<tr><td rowspan="2">앙
고
재</td><td>91
년
5
월
15
일</td><td>기안자
성명</td><td>과 장</td><td>국 장</td><td>차 관</td><td>장 관</td></tr>
<tr><td>송○○</td><td></td><td></td><td></td><td></td></tr>
</table>

외신과통제

0200

외 무 부

종 별 :

번 호 : UNW-1289 　　　　　　　　　일 시 : 91 0517 1945

수 신 : 장 관(국연,미중,기정) 사본:주트리니다드 대사:본부중계필

발 신 : 주 유엔 대사

제 목 : 안보리 문서(세인트 빈센트)

　　세인트빈센트는 아국 유엔가입을 지지하는 정부 코뮤니커 를 5.16 자 안보리문서 (S/22600) 로배포한바, 동 문서를 별첨송부함.

　　첨부:상기 안보리문서 : UNW(F)-215

　　끝

　　(대사 노창희-국장)

국기국　　1차보　　미주국　　정문국　　안기부

PAGE 1　　　　　　　　　　　　　　　　　91.05.18　　09:45 WG

　　　　　　　　　　　　　　　　　　　　외신 1과 통제관

　　　　　　　　　　　　　　　　　　　　0201

**NITED
!ATIONS**

UNW(F)-215 10517 1945
(국연.미중.기초)   총104

S

Security Council

Distr.
GENERAL

S/22600
16 May 1991

ORIGINAL: ENGLISH

LETTER DATED 16 MAY 1991 FROM THE PERMANENT REPRESENTATIVE
OF SAINT VINCENT AND THE GRENADINES TO THE UNITED NATIONS
ADDRESSED TO THE PRESIDENT OF THE SECURITY COUNCIL

On instructions from my Government, I have the honour to transmit to you
the text of a communiqué which was issued relative to the application by the
Republic of Korea to become a member of the United Nations:

"The Government of Saint Vincent and the Grenadines supports the
aspiration of the Republic of Korea to seek membership of the United
Nations during the course of this year as indicated in its memorandum
S/22455 dated 5 April 1991.

"The Government of Saint Vincent and the Grenadines firmly believes
that the admission of the Republic of Korea would not only be in
conformity with the principle of universality, but that it would also
assist in creating a better political environment for a peaceful solution
to the Korean question."

I should be grateful if you would have the text of the letter circulated
as a document of the Security Council.

(Signed) Kingsley C. A. LAYNE
Ambassador
Permanent Representative

91-15906 2326g (E)

#UNW-1289
첨부물

0202

주 과 테 말 라 대 사 관

과정 20311- 164   1991. 5. 17.

수신 장 관

참조 국제기국조약국장, 미주국장.

제목 유엔 가입 지지.

        연: GUW-159

        연호 주재국의 아국 유엔 가입 지지 공한을 별첨 송부 합니다.

    첨부: 동 공한 사본 각 1부.   끝.

            주   과   테   말   라   대

0203

Guatemala, 15 de mayo de 1991

Señor Embajador:

Tengo el honor de dirigirme a Vuestra Excelencia para referirme a su atenta nota número KGU/138/91 del 29 de abril recién transcurrido, por la cual tiene a bien comunicarme que su Ilustrado Gobierno ha decidido presentar la solicitud de la República de Corea para ingresar como Miembro Pleno a la Organización de las Naciones Unidas y al mismo tiempo solicita el apoyo del Gobierno de Guatemala para dicha aspiración.

Me permito manifestar a Vuestra Excelencia que el Gobieno de Guatemala, teniendo en cuenta las cordiales relaciones de amistad, solidaridad y cooperación que felizmente existen entre nuestros Pueblos y Gobiernos ha decidido otorgar el apoyo requerido, habiéndole dado las instrucciones correspondientes al Embajador, Representante Permanente de Guatemala ante las Naciones Unidas.

Aprovecho la ocasión para renovar a Vuestra Excelencia las seguridades de mi alta y distinguida consideración.

ALVARO ARZU
MINISTRO DE RELACIONES EXTERIORES

Excelentísimo Señor
Key-Sung Cho
Embajador Extraordinario y Plenipotenciario
de la República de Corea
Ciudad.-

0204

MMN/1r.-

외 무 부

원 본

종 별 :

번 호 : UNW-1324   일 시 : 91 0522 1800

수 신 : 장 관(국연,미중,기정)사본:주트리니다드대사:본부중계필

발 신 : 주 유엔 대사

제 목 : 안보리 문서(세인트루시아)

    세인트루시아의 아국 유엔가입을 지지하는 안보리문서 (S/22628) 가 금 5.22 자로
배포된바, 동문서를 별첨송부함.

    첨부:상기 안보리문서: UNW(F)-223

    끝

    (대사 노창희-국장)

국기국   1차보   미주국   정문국   안기부

PAGE 1

91.05.23   09:21 WG
외신 1과 통제관

0205

UNW(FR)-223 10522
(국연. 미중. 기70)

UNITED NATIONS

Security Council

총104

Distr.
GENERAL

S/22628
22 May 1991

ORIGINAL: ENGLISH

LETTER DATED 8 MAY 1991 FROM THE PERMANENT REPRESENTATIVE OF
SAINT LUCIA TO THE UNITED NATIONS ADDRESSED TO THE PRESIDENT
OF THE SECURITY COUNCIL

Upon instructions from my Government, I have the honour to inform you, in your capacity of President of the Security Council, that the Government of Saint Lucia supports fully the aspiration of the Republic of Korea to become a Member of the United Nations. Saint Lucia is of the view that the Republic of Korea's membership in the Organization would be most consistent with the principle of universality embodied in the spirit of the Charter.

In this regard, the Government of Saint Lucia supports the memorandum of the Government of the Republic of Korea contained in Security Council document S/22455 of 9 April 1991.

I should be grateful if you would have the text of this letter circulated as a document of the Security Council.

(Signed) Charles S. FLEMMING
Ambassador
Permanent Representative

91-16478 2313i (E)

#UNW-1324
청부뜩

0206

주 필 리 핀 대 사 관

주비정 700 - **0537**   1991. 5. 22.

수 신 : 장관

참 조 : 국제기구조약국장

제 목 : 아국 유엔가입

　　　　　연 : PHW-0698

　　　　　주재국이 아국 유엔가입신청시 이를 지지한다는 내용의 구상서(원본)

을 별첨 송부 합니다.

　　별 첨 : 상기 구성서 1부.　끝.

　　예고: 91.12.31(일반)

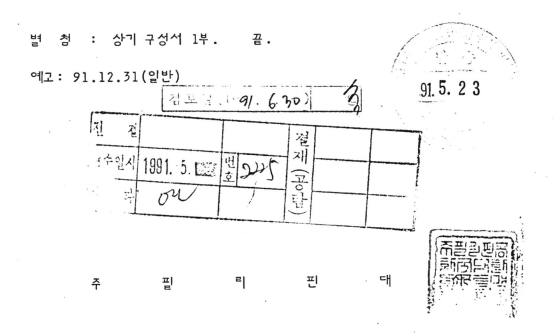

91.5.23

주 　 필 　 리 　 핀 　 대

0207

The Department of Foreign Affairs presents its compliments to the Embassy of the Republic of Korea and has the honour to refer to the latter's Note No. KPH-91-030 of 17 April 1991 regarding the Republic of Korea's application for membership in the United Nations.

The Department is pleased to inform the Embassy that, in view of the Philippines' adherence to the principle of universality of membership in the United Nations, the Philippines will support the UN membership bid of the Republic of Korea. In the same manner, the Philippines will support an application for membership in the United Nations of the Democratic People's Republic of Korea, in the event the DPRK decides to do so.

The Department of Foreign Affairs avails itself of this opportunity to renew to the Embassy of the Republic of Korea the assurances of its highest consideration.

Manila, 16 May 1991

0208

주 시 에 라 렉 음 대 사 관

주시에라 (정) 20311-120   1991. 5. 27.

수 · 신 : 장   관 (사본: 주유엔대사)

참   조 : 국제기구조약국장

재   목 : 주재국의 유엔가입 아국입장 지지 공식표명

　　　대 : EM-0009

　　　연 : SRW-0132, 0136

　　　아국의 유엔가입 입장에 대한 지지입장을 밝히는 주재국 정부(외무부)의
구상서를 금 5. 27. 수령하였기 동 부본을 별첨 송부합니다.

　　　첨   부 : 구상서 부본. 끝.

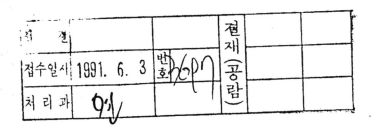

검토필(1991.6.30)

처 결			결재(공람)		
접수일시	1991. 6. 3	번호			
처리과					

주 시 에 라 렉 백 온 대 사 대

0209

The Ministry of Foreign Affairs of the Republic of Sierra Leone presents its compliments to the Embassy of the Republic of Korea in Freetown and has the honour to refer to the memorandum of the Government of the Republic of Korea dated 5th April 1991 relating to the intention of the Government of the Republic of Korea to seek admission to the United Nations Organisation during the 46th Session of the General Assembly.

The Ministry of Foreign Affairs wishes to inform the esteemed Embassy that the Republic of Sierra Leone in keeping with the principle of universality of the organisation, strongly supports the intention of the Republic of Korea to seek admission to the United Nations Organisation during the 46th Session.

The Government of the Republic of Sierra Leone believes that the presence of the Republic of Korea within the United Nations represents a further committment of the Republic of Korea to working towards facilitating the process of rapprochment on the Korean pennisula in accordance with the objectives and principles of the United Nations Charter.

The Government of the Republic of Sierra Leone hopes therefore that the Membership of South Korea in the United Nations will contribute to securing a durable peace on the Korean pennisula and the ultimate unification of the two Koreas.

The Ministry of Foreign Affairs of the Republic of Sierra Leone avails itself of this opportunity to renew to the Embassy of the Republic of Korea in Freetown the assurances of its highest consideration.

FREETOWN, 23RD MAY, 1991.

EMBASSY OF THE REPUBLIC
OF KOREA
WILBERFORCE STREET
FREETOWN

0210

외 무 부

종 별 :

번 호 : UNW-1385　　　　　　　　　일 시 : 91 0528 1800

수 신 : 장관(국연,미중,기정)사본:주파나마대사:본부중계필

발 신 : 주유엔대사

제 목 : 안보리문서(파나마)

　　아국유엔 가입을 지지하는 5.24.자 파나마 안보리문서(S/22639) 가 금 5.28 일 배포 된바, 동문서내용을 별첨 송부함.

　　첨부:상기 안보리문서: UNW(F)-228

　　끝

　　(대사 노창희-국장)

국기국	1차보	미주국	정문국	안기부

PAGE 1

UNN(西)—228 1≈28 /80

(국련, 이후, 기침) 총 2매

S

UNITED NATIONS

Security Council

Distr.
GENERAL

S/22639
24 May 1991
ENGLISH
ORIGINAL: SPANISH

LETTER DATED 17 MAY 1991 FROM THE CHARGE D'AFFAIRES A.I. OF THE
PERMANENT MISSION OF PANAMA TO THE UNITED NATIONS ADDRESSED TO
THE PRESIDENT OF THE SECURITY COUNCIL

I have the honour to transmit to you a letter from the Minister for
Foreign Affairs of the Republic of Panama, His Excellency Mr. Julio E. Linares.

I should be grateful if you could have this letter and its annex
circulated as a document of the Security Council.

(Signed) Eduardo A. HEART
Ambassador
Deputy Permanent Representative
Chargé d'affaires a.i.

91-17071 2469j (E)   /...

#UNW-1385
첨부 2—1

0212

S/22639
English
Page 2

<u>Annex</u>

<u>Letter dated 14 May 1991 from the Minister for Foreign Affairs
of Panama addressed to the President of the Security Council</u>

I have the honour to inform you that the Republic of Panama supports the
aspiration of the Republic of Korea to be admitted to membership in the United
Nations.

(<u>Signed</u>) Julio E. LINARES
Minister

2-2

0213

문서번호	기호	중동일720-	협조문용지	결	담 당	과 장	국 장
		175	(720-2327)	재			
시행일자		1991. 6. 10.					
수 신		국제기구조약국장	발 신		중동아프리카국장	(서명)	
제 목		바레인 국왕 친서					

       강영훈 특사편에 91.5.8. 바레인 국왕에게 전달한바 있는

대통령의 친서에 대한 ISA 바레인 국왕의 답신(주바레인대사 전문

BHW-0310 내용)을 별첨 송부하니 업무에 참고 하시기 바랍니다.

      첨 부 : 바레인 국왕 친서 사본 1부. 끝.

0214

May 21, 1991

Your Excellency,

We received with deep concern your letter dated 25th April 1991 conveyed by your special envoy, former Prime Minister, Mr. Young-Hoon Kang, during his recent visit to the State of Bahrain.

We would like to express our appreciation for the sentiments expressed therein for the victory achieved by the Allied forces in the Liberation of Kuwait. We highly value the important role played by the Republic of Korea in their readiness to cooperate and participate actively in the economic rehabilitation and to ensure peace and stability in the region.

Prompted by the existing strong ties between our two countries, and the important role being played by the Republic of Korea on the international level, the State of Bahrain looks with great concern and sympathy to your desire in seeking the United Nations' Membership, and we totally support it.

We also look forward to seeing the day which heralds the reunification of the Korean peninsula, the cherished desire of all Korean people, which to be sure, will contribute positively in enhancing peace and stability in your region.

Accept, Excellency, my highest consideration.

ISA BIN SALMAN AL-KHALIFA
AMIR OF THE STATE OF BAHRAIN

His Excellency,
Roh Tae Woo
President of the
Republic of Korea

0215

بسم الله الرحمن الرحيم

۲۱ مايو ۱۹۹۱م

صاحـــب الفخـــامـــة روه تـــاى وو
رئيـــس جمهوريـــة كـوريـا المــوقــر

تسلمنـا بوافر التقديـر رسالتكم المؤرخة فى الخامس والعشرين من شهـر
ابريل ۱۹۹۱ ، والتى نقلها الينا المبعوث الخاص لفخامتكم سعادة السيد يانغ
هـون كانغ رئيس وزراء جمهورية كوريا السابق اثنـاء لقائنا به خـلال زيارتـه
لدولة البحرين .

واذ نشكركم على ماعبرتم عنـه من مشاعـر طيبة بمناسبة الانتصار الذى
حققته القوات المشتركة فى حرب تحريـر دولة الكويت ، فانه لايسعنا هنا الا
ان نقدر الدور الذى تقـوم بـه جمهوريـة كوريا واستعدادهـا للتعاون والمشاركة
فى الجهـود الدوليـة الهادفة لضمان الاستقرار واعادة البنـاء الاقتصادى فى هذا
الجزء من العالم .

وانطلاقا مـن الروابـط المتينـة القائمـة بيـن بلدينـا ، وتقديـرا للـدور الهام
الذى تقـوم بـه جمهورية كوريا على المستوى الدولى ، فان دولة البحرين تنظر
بتعاطف كبيـر واهتمام بالـغ الى الرغبة التـى اعربتم عنها فى رسالتكم بطلب
الانضمام الى عضوية المنظمة الدولية ، وانها ستؤيد طلبكم تأييدا تاما .

كمـا ونتطلـع لليـوم الذى تتوحد فيـه شبه الجزيرة الكورية ، أمل الشعب
الكورى قاطبة ، كى يكون ذلك عامـلا فى تعزيز السلم والامن والاستقرار فى
تلك المنطقة .

وتقبلوا فخامتكم بقبول اسمى اعتبارى ،،،

عيسى بن سلمان آل خليفة
أمير دولة البحرين

0216

관리 번호	91 -3885

협 조 문 용 지

분류기호 문서번호	국연 2031- 238	(2179-80)
시행일자	1991. 6. 17.	
수 신	중동아프리카국장	발 신
제 목	코트디브와르 외상 서한	

결 재	담 당	과 장	국 장

국제기구조약국장   (서명)

　
코트디브와르의 Essy Amara 외무장관은 아국의 유엔가입

지지를 요청하는 장관님 서한에 대하여 별첨 회신서한을 송부

하여 온 바, 업무에 참고하시기 바랍니다.   (5.16.字)

첨부 : 코트디브와르 외무부 공한 및 Essy Amara 외상서한

　　　 각 1부. 끝.

예고 : 91.12.31.일반

검 토 필 (1991 . 6. 30)

0217

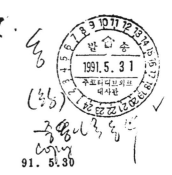

주 코트디브와르 대사관

91. 5. 30

주 코트디 (정) 720- 146.

수 신 : 외무부 장관

참 조 : 국제기구 조약국장

제 목 : 외상앞 서한

대 : 국연 2031-405

연 : IVW-0281

연호 ESSY AMARA 주재국 외상의 외무장관앞 5.16자 답신서한을 별첨과 같이 송부합니다.

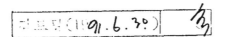

첨 부 : 상기 답신서한 . 끝.

	결			정재(공람)		
접수일자	1991. 6. 10	번호	2338			
처리과						

일반문서로 재분류 (1991. 12. 31.)

주 코트디브와르 대사관

0218

MINISTERE
DES AFFAIRES ETRANGERES

No 4528 /AE/AP/OI-13

17 MAI 1991

     Le Ministère des Affaires Etrangères de la République de Côte d'Ivoire présente ses compliments à l'Ambassade de la République de Corée à Abidjan et a l'honneur de lui faire parvenir ci-joint, un pli fermé adressé à Son Excellence Monsieur le Ministre des Affaires Etrangères de la République de Corée par Son Excellence Monsieur le Ministre des Affaires Etrangères de la République de Côte d'Ivoire.

     Le Ministère des Affaires Etrangères de la République de Côte d'Ivoire remercie l'Ambassade de la République de Corée à Abidjan de son aimable collaboration et saisit cette occasion pour lui renouveler les assurances de sa haute considération.

AMBASSADE DE LA REPUBLIQUE DE COREE

A B I D J A N

0219

*Ministère
des Affaires Etrangères*

Le Ministre

République de Côte d'Ivoire
Union - Discipline - Travail

Abidjan, le ....

N° 068 /AE/AP/OI-13

CONFIDENTIEL

Monsieur le Ministre,

J'ai l'honneur d'accuser réception de la lettre par laquelle vous sollicitez l'appui du Gouvernement ivoirien à la décision du Gouvernement coréen de demander son admission à l'Organisation des Nations Unies (ONU).

La Côte d'Ivoire, pays épris de paix, reste profondément attachée au principe d'universalité et autres objectifs de l'Organisation des Nations Unies qu'elle considère comme le cadre par excellence de coopération et de reconciliation entre les communautés humaines.

En conséquence, mon Gouvernement vous apportera volontiers son soutien pour votre entrée à l'ONU.

Je saisis par ailleurs cette occasion pour réaffirmer la volonté de mon pays de s'associer à tous les efforts de la Communauté Internationale visant au maintien de la paix, de la sécurité internationale ainsi qu'au respect des Droits de l'Homme.

J'ai été sensible aux mots aimables que vous avez bien voulu adresser à mon endroit ainsi qu'à mon pays.

SON EXCELLENCE MONSIEUR
LEE SANG-OCK
MINISTRE DES AFFAIRES ETRANGERES

S E O U L

REPUBLIQUE DE COREE

.../...

0220

Je vous prie d'accepter les voeux les meilleurs qu'en retour, je forme pour le bonheur de votre Excellence ainsi que pour la prospérité du vaillant peuple de la République de Corée.

Je vous prie d'agréer, Monsieur le Ministre, l'assurance de ma haute considération.

0221

외교문서 비밀해제: 남북한 유엔 가입 1
남북한 유엔 가입 총회결안 추진 및 기본입장 각서

초판인쇄 2024년 03월 15일
초판발행 2024년 03월 15일

지은이 한국학술정보(주)
펴낸이 채종준
펴낸곳 한국학술정보(주)
주 소 경기도 파주시 회동길 230(문발동)
전 화 031-908-3181(대표)
팩 스 031-908-3189
홈페이지 http://ebook.kstudy.com
E-mail 출판사업부 publish@kstudy.com
등 록 제일산-115호(2000. 6. 19)

ISBN 979-11-6983-942-6 94340
       979-11-6983-945-7 94340 (set)